Malthouse Monographs on Africa

Editor: Dafe Otobo, DPhil (Oxford),
Professor, University of Lagos, Lagos, Nigeria

Advisory Editorial Board

Professor Adele Jinadu, Centre for Advanced Social Science, Port Harcourt, Nigeria.
Professor John Ohiorhenuan, UNDP, New York, USA.
Professor Eddie Webster, University of Witwatersrand, Johannesburg, South Africa
Gavin Williams, St Peter's College, University of Oxford, UK.

Malthouse Monographs on Africa

Malthouse Monographs on Africa are peer-reviewed works on Africa covering the six main areas of a) social sciences and development studies; b) history, law and international relations; c) environmental and agricultural studies; d) gender, refugee and conflict studies; e) strategic and defence studies; and f) labour and trades unions.

The monographs are intended to provide an arena for free contestation of ideas and as outlet for research and empirical studies on Africa in the areas indicated above. The monographs thus have no links with, nor funded by, any government or political party. Nor do the views expressed in them represent those of the editorial board.

Works for consideration may be of purely theoretical, or historical or applied in nature or policy-oriented. Such may be sent directly to the Editor as electronic files (dafeotobo2002@yahoo.co.uk) in Microsoft Word Rich Text format, or to the publishers (malthouse_press@yahoo.com}. Diskettes and hardcopies may also be sent to the publishers at the address on the imprint page. The aim is to publish accepted works within three months.

Malthouse Monographs on Africa
Numbers 1 – 10

Guest Series Editor: Dayo Oluyemi-Kusa,
*Director, External Conflict Prevention & Resolution,
Institute for Peace and Conflict Resolution, The
Presidency, Abuja, Nigeria*

- Rotimi T. Suberu, *Institutional structure and process of government in Nigeria, 1985-1993*
- R. A. Akindele, *Federalism under General Babangida's administration in Nigeria*
- Dele Olowu & Kunle Awotokun, *Local government and the IBB administration*
- Cyril Obi, *The Nigerian private sector under adjustment and crisis 1985-1993*
- Bola A. Akinterinwa, *General Ibrahim Babangida's legacy: the domestic and international dimensions*
- Nereus I. Nwosu, *Nigeria's foreign policy under General Babangida*
- Antonia T. Oko-Osi, *Corruption and corrupt practices: institutionalization and legitimation under the Babangida Administration*
- Oyeleye Oyediran & Babafemi Badejo, *The military and democracy in Nigeria: the Political Bureau Report*
- Adekunle Amuwo, *Politics of the annulment of June 12 presidential election in Nigeria*

Malthouse Press Limited
43 Onitana Street, Off Stadium Hotel Road,
Surulere, Lagos, Lagos State
E-mail: malthouse_press@yahoo.com
malthouse_lagos@yahoo.co.uk
Tel: +234 (01) -773 53 44; 0802 364 2402

© Malthouse Monographs on Africa 2007
First Published 2007
ISBN 978 023 230 3

Distributors:
African Books Collective Ltd
Email: abc@africanbookscollective.com
Website: http://www.africanbookscollective.com

Guest Editor's comment

All the Monographs in this series attempt to explore and document events, policies and impact of the General Ibrahim Babangida-led military regime in Nigeria, covering the period 1985 to 1993. These contributions were originally for a book edited by me on that regime but other considerations, especially that of comprehensiveness of coverage of arguably the most momentous phase in Nigeria's post-Civil War socio-political development, led to the shelving of that idea. It was thought that a more useful scope or coverage might be achieved through a continuing development of Monographs on different facets of Nigerian society under this regime – a feat which may only be possible in a book so voluminous and whose cost might be such as to be out of the reach of the intended audience.

I should like to thank all the contributors who have waited this long to see their work in print, a fate that is unlikely to befall the contributors of the other titles currently in preparation. I am grateful to the publishers for including these titles in Malthouse Monographs for Africa family.

Dayo Oluyemi-Kusa

Institutional structure and process of government in Nigeria, 1985-1993

Rotimi T. Suberu, PhD
Department of Political Science
University of Ibadan
Ibadan, Nigeria

No. 1

Contents

Introduction   8
Conceptual and historical prologue   8
The development of an imperial military presidency   13
The institutions and progress of re-civilianisation   22
Redesigning the federal system   29
Conclusion   36

Introduction

This monograph probes key developments in the institutional framework and governmental processes of the Nigerian state during the eight-year military presidency and dictatorship of General Ibrahim Babangida. Three interrelated, but analytically distinguishable, aspects of the country's governmental institutions and processes during this period are examined, namely, the institutional structure and politics of the military government or regime, the institutions and processes of Babangida's democratic transition project, and the institutional structure and dynamics of the federal system. This discussion is appropriately preceded by an elucidation of relevant conceptual and historical issues.

Conceptual and historical prologue

Political institutions refer to the formal organisational machinery and procedural norms through which political relationships or processes are regularized, mediated or conducted. These institutions include the executive, legislative and juridical structures of the state machinery, as well as constitutions, legal systems, party systems and the like.[1]

---

[1] Francis Fukuyama, 'The Primacy of Culture', *Journal of Democracy*, Vol. 6, No. 1, (1995), p. 7

A lively debate persists in political science regarding the importance of political institutions, and the processes that give concrete expression to them, in shaping the trajectory of fundamental socio-political outcomes and processes. An 'old institutionalism' in political studies regarded the institutional structure of the state as providing the primary nexus or pivot around which political life revolves. However, subsequent theories of political science, dating from the behavioural revolution of the early and mid-twentieth century, assigned little explanatory importance or socio-political significance to the autonomous role of political institutions. According to these theories, formally organized political institutions are simply the arenas within which political behaviour occurs. This behaviour, it is argued, is driven not by the institutions themselves, but by such relatively more fundamental, non-institutional factors as civil society, political culture and economic development.[2] Indeed, in a recent restatement of the non-institutionalist thesis, Francis Fukuyama bluntly contends that 'the real, difficulties affecting the quality of life in modern democracies have to do with social and cultural pathologies that seem safely beyond the reach of institutional solutions, and hence of public policy.'[3]

But James G. March and Johan P. Olsen contend that, in recent years, a 'new institutionalism' has appeared in political studies. According to them:

> Without denying the importance of both the social context of politics and the motives of individual actors, the new institutionalism insists on a more

[2] James G. March and Johan P. Olsen, 'The New Institutionalism: Organisational Factors in Political Life,' *American Political Science Review*, Vol. 78 (September 1984), p. 734.

[3] Fukuyama, 'The Primacy of Culture', p. 9.

autonomous role for political institutions. The state is not only affected by society but alto affects it. Political democracy depends not only on economic and social conditions but also on the design of political institutions.[4]

A major reason for the resurgence and influence of institutionalist perspectives in recent comparative political studies involves the recognition that, whereas non-institutional factors like culture and economics are not immediately alterable, political institutions can be created or manipulated fairly rapidly and ingeniously in response to immediate needs, problems or challenges. This insight is especially apposite for developing countries where non-institutional factors are almost always hostile to the creation or consolidation of a stable and legitimate political order. As Larry Diamond, Juanz Linz and S.M. Lipset, for example, succinctly put it,

> ...constitutional and party structures play an important role in shaping the conflict-regulating capacity of democratic systems. While these conditions of political structure are not intrinsically necessary for stable democracy, they become particularly significant as social, cultural and economic conditions become less favourable.[5]

Nigeria's recent political history is replete with instances, of the pragmatic creation and transformation of constitutional and institutional structures in the search for a

---

[4] March and Olsen, 'The New Institutionalism,' p. 738.
[5] L. Diamond, J. Linz, and S.M. Lipset, 'Introduction' in L. Diamond, J. Linz and S.M. Lipset (eds.), *Politics in Developing Countries: Comparing Experiences With Democracy* (Boulder, C O: Lynne Rienner Publishers, (1990), p. 5.

viable political order. At the lime of her independence from Britain in October 1960, three features dominated Nigeria's politico-institutional landscape. The first was a civilian constitutional regime in which political authority was legally vested in the elected representatives of the people. The second feature of Nigeria's institutional landscape in the immediate post-independence era was a profoundly defective federal structure, which consisted of a relatively weak national government and three (later four) large and powerful, but unequal and ethnically unwieldy, regional governments. The third feature was a parliamentary political system, modelled closely on the British Westminster paradigm, with a bicephalous federal executive that included a ceremonial president and an elected prime minister.

The violent overthrow of Nigeria's First Republic (1960-1966) in January 1966 overturned all the three aforementioned institutional features of the immediate post-independence era. In the first place, the discredited civilian political class was replaces by a military regime whose institutional structures and processes differed radically from those of the civilian political system. The hierarchical, centralized and relatively cohesive institutional structure of the military establishment though never completely immune from countervailing pressures in the wider Nigerian society, contrasted sharply with the rancour and anarchy of the civilian regime. Among other consequences, this distinctive structural advantage enabled the military, and their collaborators in the federal bureaucracy and among the civilian political class, to embark on a decisive and comprehensive programme of political engineering and institutional redesigning.

By far the most important institutional innovation and structural achievement of the first phase (1966-1979) of military rule in Nigeria was the replacement of the grossly lopsided regional system with a more institutionally balanced federal system of multiple states. First, on the eve of the Nigeria-Biafran war in 1967, General Yakubu Gowon replaced the four regions of the defunct First Republic with twelve states. Then, in 1976, the twelve states became nineteen when Gowon's successors, Generals Murtala Mohammed and Olusegun Obasanjo, established seven additional states. Along with associated federalist reforms in the system of revenue allocation and the structure of local government, these state reorganisation exercises transformed Nigeria into a relatively more integrated, decentralized, ethnically equitable and structurally coherent federation.

These integrative federalist innovations were buttressed by the institutional changes that were enacted during the four-year (1975-1979) programme of constitutional planning and political transition that culminated in the inauguration of the 1979 Constitution for the Second Republic in October of that year. Perhaps the most significant innovation of the new constitution was the replacement of the British parliamentary model with an American-style presidential system. Another major constitutional innovation involved the requirement that the plural nature or 'federal character' of the country be reflected in the procedures for electing the president, in the formation and organisation of political parties, and in the composition and conduct of public agencies. Finally, reflecting its integrative assumptions and aspirations, the 1979 Constitution endowed the federal government with legislative competence over an omnibus range of subjects, including several subjects that had been assigned to the regional governments of the First Republic.[6]

Yet, these institutional and constitutional reforms could not save the Second Republic from systematic violation, structural, degeneration and eventual dissolution. The Republic was sacked at the end of 1983 by the Mohammed Buhari/Tunde Idiagbon military administration, which subsequently prohibited any public discussion of Nigeria's future constitution and institutions. Growing popular disenchantment with the new administration's illiberal posture provided the backdrop to the palace coup that ushered Babangida into power in August 1985. Almost immediately, Babangida embarked on an ambitious project of political engineering that, as already indicated, involved three broad institutional arenas or levels, namely, the institutional structure of military rule, the institutional framework of the re-civilianization project, and the institutional matrix of the federal system in general.

The development of an imperial military presidency

The institutional framework and associated processes of military rule under Babangida were significantly comparable to the institutional and operational modalities of previous military governments in Nigeria. These general structural modalities of military rule include the centralization of power in the national military government, the subordination of the federal system to the unified military command structure (the so-called 'command

---

[6] See C.S. Whitaker Jr., 'Second Beginnings: The New Political Framework,' *Issue*, Vol. 11 (1981), p. 10.

federalist system')[7] a formal commitment to peace, national unity, order and good or -corrective government, and the vigorous and sustained affirmation of the prerogative of the military to define and redefine Nigeria's political system including the structure of any future civilian regime.

While sharing a basic similarity or comparability with the previous practice of military rule in Nigeria, however, the Babangida era introduced some fundamental innovations into the structure and processes of military government in the country. Two of these changes were particularly striking. These were the unprecedented personalization and concentration of power in the office of the military head of state, and the move towards the institutionalization of arrangements for joint military-civilian governance (dyarchy). Both of these changes were ultimately related to General Babangida's 'power-lust' and his quest for long-term personal political ascendancy and legitimacy.[8]

Thus, on coming to power in August 1985, Babangida, in an unprecedented move, appropriated the civilian constitutional title of "president". The ostensible reason for this move was the need to realign the institutional structure of military rule in Nigeria with the constitutional practice of presidentialism. Indeed, the Babangida administration was subsequently to initiate major reforms in the civil service and local government system that similarly sought to bring the structure of these institutions into conformity with the practice of presidentialism. However, Babangida's

---

[7] See William D. Graf, *The Nigerian State* (London: James Currey, 1988), p. 134.

[8] The phrase 'power lust' is borrowed from Wole Soyinka. See Tunde Adeniran, *The Politics of Wole Soyinka* (Ibadan: Fountain Publications, 1994), p. 172.

decision to assume the title of 'president' not only hinted at his long-term political ambitions, but also provided the primary institutional prop for his emergence as the most powerful head of state in the country's history. As Adebayo Williams perceptively observed as early as December 1985, with Babangida, we have for the first time in our history the closest thing to a genuinely imperial presidency. Nobody in the history of this country has had more power vested in him.[9]

Babangida's quest for absolute power was partly underscored and facilitated by the relegation of the previous office of the Chief of Staff, Supreme Headquarters, whose incumbent is generally regarded as the *de facto* deputy head of state. Under Babangida, this office was redesigned the office of the Chief of General Staff, General Staff Headquarters, and its incumbent was no longer allowed to exercise any control over military, police and related security matters. Military matters, for instance, were now vested in the newly established office of the Joint Chiefs of Staff, under the chairmanship of the minister of defence.[10] In essence, the office of the Chief of General Staff was now left with only the purely administrative responsibility of supervising the activities of state administrations and governors.

The ostensible reason for this deliberate downplaying of the office of the *de facto* deputy head of state was the need to avoid a re-enactment of the expansion and manipulation of this office by General Tunde Idiagbon during the preceding military administration. Yet, its actual impact was to further confirm and consolidate the pre-eminent status of Babangida in the military power

---

[9] Adebayo Williams, in *Newswatch* (Lagos), 9 December 1985, p. 10.

[10] See *West Africa* (London), 9 September 1985, p. 1844.

structure. The magnitude of this presidential hegemony was poignantly dramatized in October 1986 when Babangida, in an unprecedented move, replaced Commodore Ebitu Ukiwe with Rear Admiral Augustus Aikhomu as the Chief of General Staff. What is more, throughout the life of his administration, Babangida enjoyed a personal prerogative to "appoint and remove any officer in the administration".[11]

Other initial institutional changes implemented by Babangida included the reconstitution and re-designation of the Supreme Military Council (SUC) and the Federal Executive Council (FEC) as the Armed Forces Ruling Council (AFRC) and the National Council of Ministers (NCU) respectively. The larger, and more broadly based, AFRC, in particular was ostensibly designed to ensure 'collective leadership and decision-making' as opposed to the alleged violation of the principle of collective authority and responsibility under Buhari and Idiagbon's more narrowly constituted SMC.[12] The administration's formal commitment to collective and responsive governance was further underscored by the promotion of public discussion of key national issues (e.g., the IMF debate, the Political Debate and the All-Nigerian Conference on Foreign Policy), and by the establishment of the Services Consultative Committee (SCC) and the Armed Forces Consultative Assembly (AFCA), in December 1986 and June 1989 respectively, as avenues of military-wide consultation and participation under the administration.[13]

---

[11] *West Africa* (London), 13 October 1986, p. 2145.

[12] *West Africa* (London), 2 September 1985, p. 1828; and *The Guardian* (Lagos), 2 January 1993, p. 5.

[13] For President Babangida's speeches at the inaugural sessions of the SCC and AFCA, See *Portrait of a New Nigeria: Selected Speeches of IBB* (London: Precision Press, 1-98 pp. 109 - 125.

But the superficiality and vulnerability of Babangida's institutions for collective governance was demonstrated by the dictator's *capricious relationship* with these institutions. The SCC and AFCA, for instance, remained largely moribund, and were never allowed to develop into regular components of the governmental machinery. Even the strategic AFRC suffered a virtually similar fate. Its membership was repeatedly changed by the president, who also unilaterally dissolved and reconstituted the body on at least two occasions. The national council of ministers (NCM) was similarly degraded. By the sixth anniversary of his administration in August 1991, Babangida had reshuffled the NCM seven times, and had removed or reassigned about 50 ministers.[14] During the same period, Babangida changed the military governors up to eight times, and 'appointed about 70 governors in 30 states.'[15]

But while the aforementioned institutions were being systematically undermined and weakened, the presidency was being strengthened via the proliferation of institutions appointed by the president to prosecute the government's economic reform and political transition programmes. Some of these presidential appointed and/or presidential-controlled institutions included the directorate for food, roads and rural infrastructure (DFRRI), the national directorate of employment (NDE), the technical committee on privatization and commercialization, the boards of community banks and Peoples' bank, the national revenue mobilisation, allocation and fiscal commission (NRMAFC), the national population commission (NPC), the national electoral commission (NEC), the directorate of social mobilisation for self-reliance and economic recovery

---

[14] See *Newswatch* (Lagos), 14 October 1991, p. 15.

[15] *Newswatch* (Lagos), 27 January 1992, p. 9.

(MAMSER), the centre for democratic studies (CDS), the national council on intergovernmental relations (NCIR), the presidential advisory committee (PAC), the Political Bureau, the National Guard (a military outfit) and, of course, the security agencies.[16]

The expansion and transformation of the security agencies by Babangida provide an apt illustration of the politics of institutional consolidation under the dictator's military presidency. One of Babangida's initial actions as military president involved the denunciation of the abuses of the Nigerian Security Organisation (NSO), and the announcement of a plan to reform the security establishment. Consequently, in June 1986, the NSO was replaced with three new security agencies, namely, the State Security Services (SSS), the National Intelligence Agency (NIA), and the Defence Intelligence Agency (DIA). The SSS, NIA and DIA were, respectively, vested with responsibility for intelligence within the country, international intelligence and defence-related intelligence. The office of the Co-ordinator of National Security (CONS) was also established to co-ordinate the activities of the three organisations. The CONS, as well as the heads of the three intelligence agencies, were directly responsible to the president.[17] In essence, under the pretext of reforming and sanitizing the NSO, Babangida had established a massive state security apparatus that was more overweening and intrusive, and ultimately more ruthless and repressive than the defunct NSO.

---

[16] For a fairly exhaustive account by President Babangida himself of 'institution-building' under the Babangida Administration, See *The Guardian* (Lagos), 2 January 1993. p. 5.

[17] See *West Africa* (London), 16 June 1986, p. 1286

Aside from the personalization of power, the move towards military-civilian dyarchy was the most distinguishing feature of military rule under Babangida. To be sure, all previous military administrations had delegated important political roles to civilian elements, largely as ministers or commissioners in federal and state cabinets. But the scope of civilian political participation in Babangida's government was quite unprecedented. Such massive civilian participation was officially explained in terms of the administration's liberal proclivities (military democracy) and the incremental or sequential nature of its re-civilianization programme. To many critical observers, however, the extensive involvement of civilians in the Babangida administration was simply part of an attempt to legitimize and perpetuate the dictator's military presidency.

Babangida's novel experiments in military-civilian dyarchy found expression in numerous ways. In August 1990, for instance, Babangida decided to appoint a civilian vice-president in the place of the Chief of General Staff. Consequently the erstwhile Chief of General Staff Augustus Aikhomu, was retired from the armed forces and designated as the vice-president of the federation. What is more, all serving officers holding ministerial positions were retired from the military in order to further civilianize the cabinet.[18] Similarly, civilian deputies were appointed for all state military governors. All this was followed in January 1992 by the inauguration of full-fledged civilian administrations at the state-level, even as the military continued to control the presidency and the federal government.

---

[18] See Chidi Amuta, *Prince of the Niger: the Babangida Years* (Lagos: Tanus Communications and Zomax Publications, 1992), p. 287.

The highpoint of Babangida's experiments in joint military-civilian rule involved the administrative changes that were announced in the aftermath of the abortive presidential primaries of August September 1992. The major elements of these changes, which took effect as from January 1993, included:

(i) the replacement of the AFRC with the National Defence and Security Council (NDSC), an advisory presidential body that was first established in 1986, and subsequently encoded in the 1989 Constitution for the aborted Third Republic as the National Defence Council (NDC) and National Security Council (NSC);

(ii) the replacement of the National Council of Ministers with an overwhelmingly civilian dominated Transitional Council, and the appointment of a civilian businessman, Chief Ernest Shonekan, as chairman of the council and head of government (in effect, a kind of prime minister);

(iii) the inauguration of the two houses of the National Assembly, the Senate and House of Representatives, which had been elected since July 1992;

(iv) the continuation of Babangida in office as the military president of the Federal Republic and Commander-In-Chief of the Armed Forces.

As succinctly described by one writer:

> The new arrangement represents a four-way structure of governance. At the zenith of the hierarchy is the president himself...followed by the NDSC (made up of 14 members, nine of whom are

> military officers]', the Transitional Council and the elected National Assembly, which has jurisdiction over nine legislative items, as opposed to the NDSCs 29 items.[19]

This unusual political arrangement was denounced by pro-democratic groups as 'Babangida's attempt to foist a hand-picked, subservient, so-called transitional council' on the nation in order 'to disguise his military dictatorship in a fashionable garb.'[20] Although Babangida denied that dyarchy was a goal of his re-democratisation programme, many critics saw the changes as a move towards full-fledged military-civilian governance, which 'is an implicit acknowledgement that the military have the (constitutional) right to rule.'[21]

Following the presidential election crisis of June 1993 and the forced abdication of Babangida the following August, new political arrangements were introduced in the country. The erstwhile civilian head of the Transitional Council became the head of an unelected, military-backed Interim National Government (ING) and titular Commander-in-Chief of the Armed Forces. The members of the ING were respectively designated as secretaries (ministers) of the various federal ministries. The full legislative powers of the National Assembly were somewhat restored.

However, this dubious and curious political contraption unravelled in November 1993 when the erstwhile defence secretary in the ING, General Sani Abacha, forced aside the civilian head of the ING, and

[19] Olugbenga Ayeni, 'The new formula,' *West Africa* (London), 11-17 January 1993, p. 8.
[20] *Newswatch* (Lagos), 30 November 1992, p. 18.
[21] *Newswatch* (Lagos), 14 December 1992, p. 17.

reintroduced full military rule. Among other consequences, the Abacha coup effectively overturned all the institutions that Babangida had put in place as part of his elaborate project of re-democratisation.

The institutions and progress of re-civilianisation

Five major features dominated the institutions and processes of Babangida's re-democratisation or re-civilianization programme. These included the programmers initially measured and methodical time-frame, the emphasis on institutional and cultural engineering as a prerequisite for democratisation, the two party system, the close regulation and supervision of the programme by the military, and the programmers relentlessly and ruinously contradictory character.

The development of a deliberate, gradual or carefully phased transition programme was a persistent concern of the Babangida government. For Babangida and his advisors, a major flaw of the previous transition programme that produced the ill-fated Second Republic (1979-83) was the hurried manner in which the programme was designed and implemented. Consequently, the Babangida administration sought to make its own re-democratization project

> a broadly spaced transition in which democratic government can proceed with political learning, institutional adjustment and a reorientation of political culture, at sequential levels of politics and

governance, beginning with local government and
ending at the federal level.[22]

Although the actual time-table of Babangida's
transition programme was largely crowded and
overloaded,[23] it was the initial quest for a measured and
methodical transition that provided the justification both for
Babangida's dubious experiments in dyarchy, and for the
postponement of the original date of the military's final
disengagement from October 1990 to October 1992. As it is
well known, this date was further extended to January 1993
and, subsequently, to August 1993.

The government's concern for 'political learning,
institutional adjustment and reorientation of political
culture' led it to institute programmes, policies and
organisations designed to secure an enabling cultural and
institutional environment for the democratisation process.
Thus, a whole generation of past politicians and office-
holders was initially banished from the transition process in
order to facilitate the emergence of a new political culture
and leadership, and protect the politics of the Third
Republic 'from unwholesome contamination and
corruption by discredited politicians.'[24] In addition, the
directorate of social mobilisation, the Centre for
Democratic Studies (CDS) and the Code of Conduct
Bureau and Tribunal were instituted, respectively,
undertake a campaign of mass political education and
reorientation, train the country's new generation of leaders
in democratic principles and praxis, and enforce probity

---

[22] *Portrait of a New Nigeria*, p. 87.
[23] See Tunji Olagunju, Adele Jinadu and Sam Oyovbaire (eds).
Transition to Democracy in Nigeria 1985-1993 (Ibadan: Safari and
Spectrum Books, 1993), p. 179.
[24] Ibid., p. 204

and accountability among public officers. Other relevant
agencies that were set up during the transition to facilitate
the processes of constitution-making, institution-building
and cultural engineering included: the 17-member Political
Bureau, whose historic report provided the intellectual
framework for the entire transition programme; the Paul
Omu Panel, a miniature committee of the AFRC and PAC,
which prepared the government's White Paper on the
Bureau's Report; the reformed national electoral
commission (NEC); the 46-member constitution review
committee, which was appointed in September 1987 to
review the 1979 Constitution and prepare a revised draft;
the 567-member Constituent Assembly, which was
convened in May 1988 to debate and ratify the draft
constitution; the Air Vice Marshall Ibrahim Alfa-led
Intergovernmental Committee on the Transition and, of
course, the two government-created political parties, the
'centre-right' National Republican Convention (NRC) and
the 'Centre-left' Social Democratic Party (SDP).

    Indeed, the mandatory two-party system is widely
acknowledged to be the most striking institutional
innovation of Babangida's transition project. Originally
recommended by the Political Bureau, the two-party system
was, among other anticipated advantages, expected to
neutralize the tendency for Nigerian politics to reduce to a
three-player ethnic game among the majority Hausa-Fulani,
Yoruba and Igbo nationalities; facilitate the emergence of
truly national parties committed to the 'national philosophy
of government'; reduce the sources of contention and
division in Nigerian politics; streamline or simplify the
processes of electoral administration; and consummate the
hitherto incipient and tentative pressures towards the
ideological crystallization of Nigerian party politics around

a broad contest between trans-regional coalitions of progressive and conservative forces. Indeed, according to the noted Nigerian diplomat and economist, Adebayo Adedeji:

> ...the search for a two-party system that is facultative of national unity and integration has been a consistent one since independence. The failure of the civilian political class to bring it about should not detract from the genius of the military in promulgating it and enabling us to realise a structure that we have been pursuing for so long.[25]

Yet, although there was considerable support for the government's imposition and legislation of the two-party system, there was intensive and massive disenchantment with the administration's decision, in October 1989, both to deny registration to any of the 13 political associations that had sought official recognition as political parties, and to assume direct responsibility for the designation, creation, organisation and funding of the two national parties. This decision to establish the SDP and NRC, *de novo*, alienated several independent groups from the transition programmer engendered deep suspicion regarding the government's intentions and - provoked profound criticisms of the government's apparent penchant for "extreme political engineering".[26]

However, the government's deep involvement and direct investment in the establishment of the two-party system was only symptomatic of another key feature of the

---

[25] See *West Africa* (London), 11-17 November 1991, p. 1878.
[26] See Oyeleye Oyediran and Adigun Agbaje, 'Two-Partyism and Democratic Transition in Nigeria,' *Journal of Modern African Studies*, Vol. 29, No. 2 (1991), p., 214.

transition programmer namely, its close and constant supervision, regulation and redefinition by the military. Indeed, Babangida had bluntly declared, while unveiling some of the processes for the transition in July 1987, that 'For the avoidance of doubt all these processes shall, at every, stage, be properly supervised by the military administration.'[27] Not surprisingly, the administration proceeded unilaterally to impose its own preferences and biases on virtually every facet of the transition programme.

Thus, the government rejected the Political Bureau's recommendations supporting a socialist socio-economic system, a unicameral federal legislature, the allocation of five per cent of legislative seats to representatives of women and labour, the representation of the military in the NPC and NEC, and only very modest (if any) changes in the internal territorial configuration of the federal system.[28] Furthermore, the administration warned the Constituent Assembly against changing the so-called 'agreed ingredients of Nigeria's political order' including federalism, presidentialism, the two-party system, the ban on old politicians, basic constitutional freedoms, and state religious impartiality.[29] Subsequently, the government expunged constitutional provisions ratified by the Assembly designating Nigeria as a welfare state, outlawing military coups "as a punishable crime at all times", and prescribing relatively high minimum age requirements for elective political offices.[30] What is more, the government re-imposed an old constitutional provision allowing a

---

[27] *Portrait of a New Nigeria*, p. 92.

[28] See *Federal Republic of Nigeria, Government's Views and Comments on the Findings and Recommendations of the Political Bureau* (Lagos: Federal Government Press, 1987).

[29] *Portrait of a New Nigeria*, p. 48.

[30] Ibid., pp. 66, 71-and 74.

maximum tenure of two terms of four years each for federal and state chief executives, in opposition to the proposals of the Bureau, CRC and CA for a single five or six-year term.[31]

Yet, these interventions or impositions by the military Junta did not necessarily enhance the quality and viability of the transition project. The government's opposition to both the anti-coup clause and the idea of single presidential and gubernatorial terms, in particular, could only have worked to undermine the country's democratic prospects, In essence, as Peter Koehn has argued, the ultimate impact of the military's over-regulation and control of the re-civilianization process was "to perpetuate major sources of political instability and to frustrate the long-term institutionalisation of civilian rule."[32]

The final feature of the transition process was, therefore, its contradictory and ultimately self-destructive character. Almost tight from its inception in 1986-87, the programme became progressively mired in contradictions, equivocations, procrastinations, violations, dislocations and manipulations.[33] Indeed, by the time of its inevitable and predictable collapse in November 1993, virtually all the major assumptions of the transition programme had been undermined or negated.

It is impossible to give an exhaustive list of the transition programmers virtually endless twists and turns, but the more poignant contradictions include the systematic repression of students, trade unions and professional

---

[31] Ibid., p. 75

[32] Peter Koehn, 'Competitive Transition to Civilian Rule: Nigeria's First and Second Experiments,' *Journal of Modern African Studies,* Vol. 27, No. 3 (1989), 430.

[33] See Rotimi T. Suberu, 'The Democratic Recession in Nigeria,' *Current History,* Vol. 93, No. 583 (May 1994), p. 214.

groups, in spite of the official commitment to re-democratisation and liberalisation; the initial banning of old breed politicians from the transition process at a time when they were being indiscriminately set free by the government from detention or imprisonment for corrupt conduct; the capricious banning, "unbanning" and "re-banning" of segments of the political class; the rejection of a role for military personnel in the NEC and NPC, despite the general move towards joint military civilian governance; the experimentation with a French-type presidential parliamentary model, despite the government's strong formal commitment to American-style presidentialism, the decision to make legislative work a part-time exercise, thereby violating the presidential principle of effective legislative checks on the-executive branch; the establishment of seven additional states in 1991, in spite of government's earlier opposition to further territorial changes; the conflation of local government boundaries with federal electoral constituencies, despite government's explicit rejection of this arrangement in its white paper on the Bureau's Report; the arbitrary sacking of elected local government councils in July 1989, in spite of government's declared commitment to the democratisation and revitalization of the local government system; the eventual dissolution of the directorate of social mobilisation, in spite of government's previous decision to make the directorate a permanent body; and the various extensions and revisions of the time-table for the re-civilianization programme.

The final and most fatal contradiction of the transition programme was, of course, Babangida's annulment of the results of the virtually flawless presidential election of June 1993. The sharp ethno-regional tensions engendered by the brazen assault on the re-democratization project served to underscore the precarious and contentious character of the Nigerian federal system as it had been developing since the inception of the Babangida administration.

Redesigning the federal system

The reform of federal institutions was an important goal and feature of General Babangida's eight-year rule. The most important element of this federalist reform agenda was the revitalization of the local government system. The Babangida government introduced constitutional, political, administrative and fiscal changes designed to alter local-state and local-federal relationships in ways that will empower local governments.[34] The more prominent of these changes included: the elaboration and entrenchment of provisions regarding the demarcation, administration, composition and election of local government areas and councils in the federal constitution; the extension of the presidential system to the local level; the abolition of state-controlled local government ministries and service commissions in order to enhance the political and administrative autonomy of the local councils; the organization of local government elections in 1987 and 1990 after over a decade of electoral inactivity at the local level; the introduction of an approved scheme of service for local government employees; the use of the local government areas (LGAs) as the basis for representation in

---

[34] Alex Gboyega, 'Protecting Local Governments from Arbitrary State and Federal Interference: What Prospects for the 1990s?' *Publics: The Journal of Federalism,* Vol. 21, No. 4 (Fall 1991), p. 47

the state and (lower) federal legislative houses; the upward review of the proportion of the Federation Account allocated to the localities from 10 to 15 and, subsequently, 20 rather than indirect or state-routed transfer of federal statutory allocations to the localities. While these reforms did not automatically produce a more viable and stable system of local government, they generally afforded enormous institutional opportunities and possibilities for the emergence of the localities as a genuine third tier of the federal administrative matrix.

A related aspect of federal reforms under the Babangida Administration involved the reorganisation of the boundaries of the local and state governments. Contrary to the recommendations both of the committee on the review of local government administration in Nigeria (the Dasuki Committee) and a majority of the Political Bureau, the Babangida administration implemented two major reorganisations of the 301 local government, structure., which structure was first instituted in 1976, overturned during the Second Republic, and then reinstated in 1984. These reorganisations increased the number of localities in the federation to 453 and 589 in May 1989 and August September 1991 respectively. Although ostensibly designed to promote political and economic decentralization, these reorganisations also engendered deep sectional contention regarding the distribution, configuration and location of the administrative headquarters of the new localities. Such sectional contention was largely fuelled by the enhanced status of the localities as centres of power and patronage, and by the somewhat capricious and contradictory manner in which the reorganisations were implemented by the government.[35]

The creation of new states was characterised by similar, if not greater, contradiction and contention. In consonance with the views of some members of the Political Bureau, the government had created Katsina and Akwa Ibom as the country's twentieth and twenty-first states in September 1987, and then prohibited further discussions of the state-issue. Yet, largely in response to renewed sectional (mainly Igbo) pressures for new states Babangida in August 1991 established nine additional states in the country to institute a thirty-state structure. However, the 1991 reorganisations provoked an unprecedented wave of sectional protests and violent demonstrations over the state-issue. Once again, the enormous sectional and politico-economic stakes-associated with state-creation, the sheer multiplicity of statehood demands, and the inconsistent or questionable approach of the government to state reorganisations, had combined to inflame sectional passions over the new state-structure. [36]

As many perceptive observers have acknowledged, an important source of the pressures for new states and localities is the character of the Nigerian revenue sharing system, particularly the heavy dependence of the sub-federal units on federally-collected mineral revenues, and the distribution of these revenues predominantly on an equivalent basis among the constituent states and

---

[35] See Rotimi T. Suberu, '1991 State and Local government Reorganizations in Nigeria,' *Travaux Et Documents*, No. 41 (1994), pp. 22-31.

[36] Ibid., pp. 1-22

localities.[37] Partly in an attempt to reform this revenue sharing system, the Babangida administration established the national revenue mobilization, allocation and fiscal commission (NRMAFC) in 1988 as a permanent agency for the effective mobilization of public revenues and the systematic investigation and application of revenue allocation principles. The commission proceeded to design a revised revenue allocation formula. This formula, which was implemented with slight modifications as from January 1990, was further revised during December-January 1991-92 and June 1992.[38]

The vertical (inter-tier) revenue sharing arrangements embodied in the final approved formula gave the federal government 48.5 % of the Federation Account, the state governments 24 per cent, the localities 20 per cent and Special Funds 7.5 %. The Special Funds included three per cent of the Federation Account allocated to the Oil Mineral Producing Areas Development. Commission (OMPADEC), which was set up in 1992 to ameliorate the grievances of restive oil-rich ethnic minority communities in the ecologically endangered and economically depressed Delta region of southern Nigeria.

The horizontal (inter-state and inter-local) sharing scheme embodied in the final revised revenue sharing formula included the following criteria and accompanying weights: equality of states, 40 per cent; population, 30 per cent; social development factor, 10 per cent; land mass and terrain, 10 per cent; and internal revenue generation effort, 10 per cent. This horizontal sharing formula deviated from

---

[37] See ibid., pp. 3-6.

[38] T. Y. Danjuma, 'Revenue Sharing and the Political Economy of Nigerian Federalism,' *The Nigerian Journal of Federalism*, Vol. 1, No. 1 (June 1994), pp. 43-68.

the recommendations of the NRMAFC, which had proposed a weight of 20 per cent for internal revenue generation effort as a way of inducing fiscal autonomy and responsibility in the states. The commission had also opted to subsume the politically controversial principle of land mass under the social development factor.[39] In essence, the government's revision of some of the recommendations of the NRMAFC would appear to have operated largely to undermine the commission's attempts to depoliticize and rationalize the country's revenue sharing system.

The use of relative population size as a factor of horizontal revenue sharing is a major source of the political explosiveness of population counts in the country. The post-independence attempts in 1962-63 and 1973 to enumerate the national population had ended in political fiasco and ethno-regional acrimony.

Consequently, since the ill-fated 1973 census exercise, all national governments had tacitly avoided the issue. But the Political Bureau saw the conduct of a national census as an indispensable component of the re-civilianization process. Consequently, the Babangida administration established the national population commission (NPC), under Decree 23 of 1989 (with retroactive effect from 1988), to undertake the enumeration of the population of the federation. A national census was subsequently conducted during late 1991. The provisional results of the census put Nigeria's population at 88.5 million people, with the old Northern region accounting for 53 per cent of this figure. Predictably, the provisional census results engendered considerable sectional opposition, litigation and allegations of, under counting, and the final figures were never released by the Babangida administration.

---

[39] Ibid., p. 61 (Table 6).

Nevertheless, the somewhat shrewd organisation of the census by the NPC, the establishment of census tribunals, the relative downgrading of the population factor in revenue allocation, and the elimination of ethnic and religious subjects from the census questionnaire, all combined to make the 1991 census results less politically contentious or statistically outrageous than the 1962-63 and 1973 counts.[40]

Aside from territorial reorganisations, revenue allocation and population enumeration, two other contentious issues featured prominently in the politics of Nigerian federalism under Babangida. These were religion and the states of the federal capital territory.

The proximate source of religious contention and polarization under Babangida was the government's surreptitious enlistment of the country in the Organisation of Islamic Conference (OIC) in 1986. Thereafter, Christian-Muslim tensions came to crystallize dangerously around such issues as the definition of Nigeria's secularity, the constitutional status of Shari'a law, the problem of ethno-religious imbalance in political and bureaucratic representation and in the allocation of public resources, the country's external relations with Israel and the Muslim world, and the fate of Muslim youths and Christian ethnic minority elites implicated in some of the sectarian disturbances that have convulsed northern Nigeria since the Kaduna State religious riots of 1987.[41] The government tried to contain some of this religious divisiveness by establishing an advisory council on religious affairs

---

[40] See, for instance, Sam Aluko, 'Reflections on the 1991 Census,' The *Guardian On Sunday* (-Lagos), 5 April 1992, p. A7.

[41] See Rotimi T. Suberu, 'The Travails of Federalism in Nigeria,' *Journal of Democracy,* Vol. 4, No. 4 (October 1993), pp. 42-43.

(ACRA), with an equal number of Christian and Muslim members, to mediate religious harmony in the country. But the commission was polarized and paralysed by disagreements between its Christian and Muslim blocs. In July 1992, Babangida approved the 'immediate establishment' of another agency for the mediation of inter-religious peace, namely, the Centre for the Propagation of Religious and Ethnic Tolerance (CENPRETO).[42] But the centre was not inaugurated until Babangida was forced to leave office in August 1993.

One of the major administrative achievements of the Babangida administration was the movement of the presidency, along with key federal ministries, to the new federal capital territory of Abuja in December 1991. But the whole question of the status of Abuja continued to provoke sharp religious and ethno-regional disagreements over such issues as the allegations of discrimination against Christians in the allocation of land in the new capital, the implications of constitutional usages and official practices that tended to portray the territory as if it "were one of the states of the federation" (making Abuja, in effect, an additional northern state), the apparent contradiction between the city's ostensible status as a virgin territory and the government's failure to resettle or compensate its original inhabitants, and the precise administrative structure of the territory. The 1988-89 Constituent Assembly (CA) appeared to have devised an ingenious formula for resolving these and related contentious issues by designating Abuja as a mayoralty under federal

---

[42] See *New Nigerian* (Kaduna), 30 July-1992, p. 24.

jurisdiction.[43] But this compromise was considerably vitiated and complicated by the government's decision to establish area councils and customary and shari'a courts, among others, for the new federal capital.[44] In essence, under the Babangida regime, the status of Abuja remained administratively hazy and sectionally contentious.

Conclusion

Babangida's legacy in the area of institutional structures and processes of governance may be described as a mixed one. The Babangida years witnessed bold and innovative attempts to restructure and redefine the institutional bases and processes of military rule, civilian governance and federalism in Nigeria. No other administration in the country's history has done so much to redesign the "institutional architecture" of the Nigerian political system. Yet, the overall value of Babangida's political reform project is questionable, if not outrightly baneful.

Under Babangida, the structure of military rule was severely distorted and degraded by the unprecedented accumulation, concentration and personalization of power in the office of the military president. As retired General Domkat Bali put it in a memorable statement, what Babangida had done was to replace the collective

---

[43] See Bala J. Takaya, 'The Status of the Federal Capital Territory, Abuja,' *The Quarterly Journal of Administration*, Vol. 24, No. 3 (April 1990), pp. 190-205.

[44] Ibid., pp. 201-205.

dictatorship of the military with the arbitrary rulership of one person.[45]

A major casualty of Babangida's quest for personal political hegemony was the elaborate project of re-democratisation launched in 1986-87. For all its grand, if often contradictory, attempts at institution-building and cultural engineering, the re-democratisation project finally collapsed tragically in 1993 after Babangida had annulled the results of a free and fair presidential election in an abortive bid to perpetuate himself in power.

Finally, while the Babangida administration initiated and implemented important decentralising and federalist reforms, the government's manipulation or mismanagement of several sensitive ethnic, regional and religious issues worked to enfeeble national unity and endanger the country's continued existence as a single federation. Although it will be too harsh to dismiss the Babangida era as an unmitigated disaster, the dictator's impact on political governance in Nigeria may be described, with some justification, as profoundly contradictory, if not poignantly disappointing.

---

[45] See *Newswatch* (Lagos), 22 January 1990, p. 15; see also Larry Diamond, 'Nigeria's Third Quest for Democracy, *Current History* (May 1991), p. 229.

Malthouse Monographs on Africa

Editor: Dafe Otobo, DPhil (Oxford),
Professor, University of Lagos, Lagos, Nigeria

Advisory Editorial Board

Malthouse Monographs on Africa

Malthouse Monographs on Africa, new on the scene, are peer-reviewed works on Africa covering the six main areas of a) social sciences and development studies; b) history, law and international relations; c) environmental and agricultural studies; d) gender, refugee and conflict studies; e) strategic and defence studies; and f) labour and trades unions.

The Monographs are intended to provide an arena for free contestation of ideas and as outlet for research and empirical studies on Africa in the areas indicated above. The monographs thus have no links with, nor funded by, any African government or political party. Nor do the views expressed in them represent those of the editorial board.

Works for consideration may be of purely theoretical, or historical or applied in nature or policy-oriented. Such may be sent directly to the Series Editor as electronic files (dafeotobo2002@yahoo.co.uk) in Microsoft Word Rich Text format, or to the publishers (malthouse_press@yahoo.com}. Diskettes and hardcopies may also be sent to the publishers at the address on the imprint page. The aim is to publish accepted works within three months.

Malthouse Monographs on Africa
Volumes 1 - 9

Guest Series Editor: Dayo Oluyemi-Kusa,
Director, External Conflict Prevention & Resolution,
Institute for Peace and Conflict Resolution, The Presidency, Abuja,
Nigeria

- Rotimi T. Suberu, *Institutional structure and process of government in Nigeria, 1985-1993*
- R. A. Akindele, *Federalism under General Babangida's administration in Nigeria*
- Dele Olowu & Kunle Awotokun, *Local government and the IBB administration*
- Cyril Obi, *The Nigerian private sector under adjustment and crisis 1985-1993*
- Bola A. Akinterinwa, *General Ibrahim Babangida's legacy: the domestic and international dimensions*
- Nereus I. Nwosu, *Nigeria's foreign policy under General Babangida*
- Antonia T. Oko-Osi, *Corruption and corrupt practices: institutionalization and legitimation under the Babangida Administration*
- Oyeleye Oyediran & Babafemi Badejo, *The military and democracy in Nigeria: the Political Bureau Report*
- Adekunle Amuwo, *Politics of the annulment of June 12 presidential election in Nigeria*

Malthouse Press Limited
43 Onitana Street, Off Stadium Hotel Road,
Surulere, Lagos, Nigeria
E-mail: malthouse_press@yahoo.com
malthouse_lagos@yahoo.co.uk
Tel: 01-773 53 44, 0802 364 2402

© Malthouse Monographs on Africa 2007
First Published 2007
ISBN 978 023 239 7

Distributors:
African Books Collective Ltd
Email: abc@africanbookscollective.com
Website: http://www.africanbookscollective.com

Guest Editor's comment

All the Monographs in this series attempt to explore and document events, policies and impact of the General Ibrahim Babangida-led military regime in Nigeria, covering the period 1985 to 1993. These contributions were originally for a book edited by me on that regime but other considerations, especially that of comprehensiveness of coverage of arguably the most momentous phase in Nigeria's post-Civil War socio-political development, led to the shelving of that idea. It was thought that a more useful scope or coverage might be achieved through a continuing development of Monographs on different facets of Nigerian society under this regime – a feat which may only be possible in a book so voluminous and whose cost might be such as to be out of the reach of the intended audience.

I should like to thank all the contributors who have waited this long to see their work in print, a fate that is unlikely to befall the contributors of the other titles currently in preparation. I am grateful to the publishers for including these titles in Malthouse Monographs for Africa family.

Dayo Oluyemi-Kusa

Federalism under General Babangida's administration in Nigeria

R. A. Akindele
Retired Research Professor,
Nigerian Institute of International Affairs
Victoria Island, Lagos
Nigeria

No. 2

Contents

Introduction   45
On the concepts of federalism and military governance   46
The operation and practical working of Nigeria's
  Political system, 1985-1993   56
Conclusion   73

Introduction

Military rule in federal political systems poses structural problems and definitional crisis for the theory and practice of federalism. One view has it that federalism and praetorian governance are antithetical and incompatible.[46] In support of this hypothesis, it is conventional to argue that, in theory and practice, the military is not only hierarchically structured for the performance of its responsibilities but also venerates and fertilizes the command-and-obedience culture, both of which are transparently alien to the spirit and principles of non-centralization, democratic control and responsibility, oppositional politics and autonomy which underpin and characterize the doctrine and technique of federalism. While emphasizing the crucial importance of distinguishing between theory and practice and insisting that the question of compatibility be addressed not just in relation to form and theory of federalism but more importantly also in relation to the practical working and operation of the federal arrangement, another view holds that federalism and military rule can be congruently and symbiotically compatible.[47] My purpose in here is to revisit the incompatibility hypothesis, using evidence from the period

---

[46] R.A. Akindele, "Nigeria in the Global Market of Experiments in Federalism," in J.I. Elaigwu and R.A. Akindele (eds.), *Foundations of Nigerian Federalism*, 1960-1995 (Abuja, FCT: National Council on Intergovernmental Relations, 1996), ch. 1; Ivo D. Duchacek, "Antagonistic Cooperation: Territorial and Ethnic Communities," *Pubius: The Journal of Federalism*, vol. 7, No. 4 Fall 1977.

[47] Sam Egite Oyovbaire, *Federalism in Nigeria: A Study in the Development of the Nigerian State* (London: Macmillan Publishers Ltd., 1985; J. Isawa Elaigwu, "Military Rule and Federalism in Nigeria," in J. Isawa Elaigwu and R.A. Akindele (eds), *op. cit.*,

1985-1993, and argue that the Nigerian political system under General Babangida's military regime could not, and did not, in a true sense, operate as a *federal* system of government. Rather, it operated essentially as a decentralized unitary system while masquerading itself falsely and deceptively as a federal political system. For, in the words of Olatokunbo Awolowo-Dosunmu,

> ...[g]iven the nature of the military as a hierarchical and centralizing institution, a large does of unitarist accretion would appear to have been infused into the Nigerian federal system, so much so that any casual observer would wonder and worry about the integrity and survivability of the federal structure in the face of such a protracted [military] onslaught.[48]

The regimes of General Buhari and Babangida slaughtered and buried federalism in the praetorian environment of imposed, centralized and authoritarian military rule that followed the Shagari administration (1979-1983).

On the concepts of federalism and military governance

Students of military rule in federal political systems need to proceed by recognizing and addressing the pertinent point made and conceptual dilemma identified by Bayo Adekanye, which is that:

> ...military organization and federal society are two fundamentally different kinds of political

---

[48] Olatokunbo Awolowo-Dosunmu, "Observations on Nigerian Federalism," *Nigerian Journal of Federalism*, Vol. 1, No. 1 June 1994, p. 180

organizations. The former is based on unitary command concentrated authority specialization, hierarchy, discipline, continuous communications and *esprit de corps*; the latter is characterized by plural leadership, dispersed authority, separation of function, plural relations, compromise, communication discontinuities and cultural dissensus.[49]

Those of them who do not see any misnormality or incongruity in the concept of 'military federalism' or of 'command-federalist system' are, to say the least, duty-bound by the usual imperative of conceptual clarification and explication to assure their colleagues in the opposing camp, who disagree with them, that a marriage of federalism and military rule does not and can neither strain nor over-stretch the principle and concept of federalism towards an internal credibility crisis of definition and identify. But since both groups of scholars share the burden of proof and explanation of their respective positions, my primary and immediate purpose in this section is to restate and explicate the principle of federalism and concept of praetorian governance in order to show that both are theoretically incompatible.

As a political and constitutional technology for mediating and reconciling the conflicting demands of unity and diversity, of self-determination and integration and of self-rule and shared-rule, federalism involves a legally guaranteed and protected *division* of legislative powers and responsibilities between two levels government, both of which operate directly on the people in a society where

---

[49] J. Bayo Adekanye, "Military Organisation and Federal Society," *Quarterly Journal of Administration*, Vol. XVI, Nos. 1 & 2, 1981/82, pp. 3-23

significant diversities are, to a large extent, territorially demarcated and grouped. Under the constitutional structure of federalism, each level of government has a separate and autonomous existence; each level of government has at least a field of legislation over which it alone is not only competent to exercise decision-making authority but over which it also recognizes no higher authority within the federation, except in a war situation and circumstances of a grave national emergency.[50] Thus, as Ben Nwabueze has persuasively pointed out

> [a]n arrangement, such as existed in Nigeria under the military regime which legally obliges one government to accept directives from another on the conduct of its affairs is not federalism in the true sense of the word.[51]

It is prefectorial administration, which is incompatible with federalism.[52] Equally important is the fact that the federal principle requires the supremacy of a written constitution which should not and must not be unilaterally altered by one level of government. To assert, as K. C. Wheare did in his classic definition, that the federal principle is "the method of dividing powers so that the general and regional governments are each, within a sphere,

---

[50] For the classic formulation of the federal principle, see K.C. Wheare, *Federal Government*, (4th Edition; London: Oxford University Press, 1963). See also S. Rufus Davis, *The Federal Principle* (Berkeley: University of California Press, 1978).

[51] B.O. Nwabueze, *Federalism in Nigeria under the Presidential Constitution* (London: Sweet & Maxwell, 1983), p.1

[52] Daniel J. Elazar, "Is Federalism Compatible with Prefectorial Administration? *Publius: The Journal of Federalism*, Vol. 11, No. 2 Spring 1981, pp. 3-22

coordinate and independent"[53] does not carry the implication that both levels of government in the federal system cannot be interdependent. As a matter of fact, the point has been well made by M.J.C. Vile that "it is [the] combination of genuine *independence* with genuine *interdependence* which makes the federal state and distinguishes it from the merely decentralized state..."[54] What Wheare's definition underscores is that neither level of government is legally subordinate to the other in the performance of the legislative duties constitutionally allocated to it.

Constitutional federalism certainly rests squarely and congruently on a conducive and supportive political culture and a systemic environment of liberal democracy. As K.C. Wheare puts it,

> [d]ictatorship, with its one-party government and its denial of free election, is incompatible with the working of the federal principle. Federalism demands forms of government which have the characteristics usually associated with democracy or free government. There is a wide variety in the forms which such government may take, but the main essentials are free election and a party system, with its guarantee of a responsible opposition.[55]

It is difficulty to see how federalism can survive, let alone grow luxuriantly, under a non-democratic and

---

[53] Wheare, *op. cit.*, p. 10

[54] Quoted in L. Adele Jinadu, "Federalism and Democracy: Debate and Its Lessons," in S. Egite Oyovbaire (ed.), *Democratic Experiment in Nigeria: Interpretive Essays* (Benin City: Omega Publishers Limited, 1987), p. 48

[55] Wheare, *op. cit.*, p. 47

authoritarian regime, military or civilian, no matter how benevolent the authoritarian regime is and no matter how rigorously it attempts to presumptuously adapt itself to the spirit, logic and political culture of federalism.

Military rule is certainly a special category of authoritarian and dictatorial governance which is now widely regarded as an anachronism. Even if it is benevolent, it inherently prescribes certain forms of action and behaviour and typically exhibits certain traits which cumulatively result in the institutionalization of an incompatible bed-fellow relationship between it and federal governance. The military, as an institution, venerates the principles of hierarchy of authority and of unity of command, both of which jointly dignify and reify the values of hierarchical domination and centralized authority, and consequently deny the functionality of political dissent and oppositional politics. Democratic governance, democratic responsibility and democratic control cannot and do not exist in a praetorian political order. Besides, enforcing public accountability inherently sometimes poses a special problem under military rule:

> Thus, it is sometimes argued that an authoritarian one-party, one-junta, or one-man regime, which by definition concentrates all political power in the hands of the group at one central point, is incompatible with the federal concept of divided power.[56]

But, as Adele Jinadu has pointed out,

> [i]f federalism is…a matter of the non-centralization of authority and the correlative dispersal of centres and levels of authority, it should… be obvious why

---

[56] Ivo D. Duchacek, "Antagonistic Cooperation: Territorial and Ethnic Communities," *Publius: The Journal of Federalism*, Vol. 7, No. 43 Fall 1977, p. 14

theoretically it is to be expected that there should
be a close link between it and democracy.[57]

It is important to bear in mind that the values of power-
sharing, compromise, negotiation and consensus which
federalism cherishes very dearly[58] usually suffer from
trivialization and marginalization, if not outright denial, in
the political attitude and behaviour of self-appointed
military leadership reared in the authoritarian political
tradition and culture of coercion, command and obedience.
Authoritarian ethics and dictatorial tradition which
transparently and customarily accompany military rule
certainly do constitute a special problem for the survival of
constitutional federalism, a fundamental difficulty which
flows from their conceptual incompatibility and incongruity
as a basis for the organization and management of political
order in any federal society. The answer to Rivero's
pungent question, "[d]oes democracy increase the chances
of federalism?"[59] is unambiguously in affirmative; which
explains why, in the words of Daniel Elazar,

[t]he federal structures occasionally adopted by
non-democratic systems must generally be

---

[57] L. Adele Jinadu, "Federalism and Democracy: Debate and Its
Lessons," in Egite Oyovbaire (ed), *Democratic Experiment in
Nigeria: Interpretive Essays* (Benin City: Omega Publishers Limited,
1987), p. 49
[58] Daniel J. Elazar, *Exploring Federalism* (Tuscaloosa: The University
of Alabama Press, 1987), p. 181
[59] J. Rivero, "Introduction to a Study of the Development of Federal
Societies," *International Social Science Bulletin*, Vol. 4, No. 1 1952,
p. 26 Quoted in L. Adele Jinadu, "Federalism and Democracy:
Debate and Its Lessons," in S. Oyovbaire (ed), *Democratic
Experiment in Nigeria: Interpretive Essays* (Benin City: Omega
Publishers Limited, 1987), p. 40

considered 'window dressing' except in so far as
their injection may serve as a democratizing
force.[60]

There is absolutely no doubt that the notion of military
rule in a supposedly federal polity certainly represents a
drift away from the authenticity of the theory of federal
democratic governance, and is bound to cripple and
disfigure federalism as a particular technique for managing
the peculiar problems of those societies where significant
diversions are territorially grouped. As Admiral Aikhomu
correctly put it, "the cardinal principle of federalism is
opposed to the centralized unitary style of administration
which is often the course for a military regime."[61]

The constitutional structure of Nigeria's political system, 1985-1993

In this monograph, evidence will be adduced to support the
view that, under General Babangida, as in the preceding
military regimes before him, military rule took the Nigerian
political system away from its purported federalist orbit,
consequently resulting in or at least evidencing the
existence of a huge credibility crisis in the policy-makers
thinking and perception of what federalism does really
mean.

One of the first acts of General Babangida on his
assumption of duty in August 1985 as head of the country's

---

[60] Elazar, *Exploring Federalism*, p. 186
[61] A. A. Aikhomu, "Federal-State Relations under Military
Governments, 1985-1992," *Nigerian Journal of Federalism*, Vol. 1,
No. 1 June 1994, p. 10

fifth military regime was the promulgation of Decree No. 17 of 1985 which constituted the first peremptory norm and legal foundation for the practical operation of Nigeria's 'command-federalist system. Decree No. 17 of 1985, titled *Constitution (Suspension and Modification) (Amendment) Decree 1985*, amended General Buhari's *Constitution (Suspension and Modification) Decree 1984*. Although the unsuspended provisions of the *Constitution of the Federal Republic of Nigeria, 1979* were to continue in operation, certain aspects of them were further modified. Of particular interest of Nigerian federalism are the sections that redesigned and indeed fundamentally amended the division of powers between the two levels of government under General Babangida's military regime. Succinctly summarized, Decree No. 17 of 1985 empowered the federal military government "to make laws for the peace, order and good government of Nigeria or any part thereof with respect to any matter whatsoever." Isawa Elaigwu has perceptively observed that:

> ...[t]echnically this provision makes the FMG [federal military government] the sole repository of power in the State. This violates the federal principle of non-centralization of power among the component federal units. Legally, Nigeria was and is unitary under military rule.[62]

Quite understandably, faithful to the true tradition of federalism and as expected, the military governments of the states were expressly prohibited by Decree No. 17 of 1985 from making laws with respect to any matter included in the Exclusive Legislature List reserved to the federal military government. But military rule shows its praetorian

---

[62] Elaigwu, *loc. cit.*,

instincts and reveals its near-totalitarian inclination when the decree prohibited the state governments from making laws with respect to any matter in the Concurrent Legislative List except with the prior consent of the federal military government. Evaluated in the light of the true spirit and legal culture of federalism, this provision expressly underscores the subordination and indeed the inferiority of the state governments to the 'federal' military government. It would have been sufficient to say as is usually the case, that the laws of the 'federal' military government supersede those made by state military government over matters in the Concurrent Legislative List if both laws conflict. To say that a state military governor had power "to make laws for the peace, order and good government of that state" on residual matters not enumerated in the two schedules of enumerate legislative powers is a euphemistic formalism and window dressing that has to be understood and interpreted in the context of the restrictions which the decree imposed upon him as the chief executive of the state government. There is absolutely no doubt that Decree No. 17 of 1985, which along with the unsuspended provisions of the Constitution of the Federal Republic of Nigeria, 1979 was the central legal basis for governance under General Babangida's military administration, expanded and consolidated the neo-imperial legislative domination of the central government. It moved the Nigerian polity away from the realities of federal power-sharing while preserving only its hollow and cosmetic form. What Sam Oyovbaire said of the over-tilting of the balance of power during Nigeria's third military regime is also true of the fifth military regime of General Babangida:

> ...the balance of power, institutionally and politically, was clearly over-tilted in favour of the

centre *with the states as more or less tolerable elongations of the Supreme Military Council.*[63]

The greater truth is not just that the central government under General Babangida's military regime was preponderantly legislatively stronger than the governments of the constituent states, accurate as this observation may be, but that the state governments were subordinately dependent upon, existed at the pleasure of and were under the firm control of the central government which illegally acquired the constitutional prerogative and capacity to unilaterally change the fundamental law of Nigeria and to allocate legislative responsibilities as it pleased. Equally relevant is the fact that, like Section 6 of the historic Decree No. 1 of 1966, promulgated by General Aguiyi-Ironsi, and Section 5 of General Buhari's Decree No. 1 of 1984, decree No. 17 of 1985 - *Constitution (Suspension and Modification) (Amendment) Decree 1985* (which amended Decree No. 1 of 1984) - retained the following provision which is at variance with the principle of federalism: "[n[o question as to the validity of this or any other Decree or of any Edict shall be entertained by any court of law in Nigeria." In effect, under General Babangida's administration, what both the 'federal' military government and the state governments could do not only lay exclusively in the hands of the Armed Forces Ruling Council (AFRC), the highest legislative and decision-making body in the country as well as an arm of the central government, but could not also be questioned, as the federal principle conventionally describes and insists, by the third arm of government, the judiciary, which is the primary arbiter of

---

[63] Oyovbaire, *op. cit.*, pp. 111-112 (Emphasis mine)

the federal system. Yet, as Ben Nwabueze has reminded us, in any true constitutional federalism:

> [a] supreme constitution binding the general and regional governments to the terms of the federal arrangement in turn implies, as a corollary, that the power to amend it must not be lodged in either alone. The power must be given either to both together or to some authority external to both of, them, e.g. the people at a referendum, or to them in association with an external 'body.[64]

This requirement of constitutional federalism was not respected but was, in fact, ignored with contempt under General Babangida's military regime.

The operation and practical working of Nigeria's political system, 1985-1993

Students of government and politics in Nigeria between 1985 and 1993 who are pre-occupied with the mutual impact of federalism and praetorian governance are often advised to move away from the question of *form* and *theory* to the *practice* and *working* of the so-called federal arrangement since, in their view, ably expressed by Sam Oyovbaire,

> [f]ederalism...is about dependence and autonomy of the state vis-à-vis the central government in the acquisition and use of power; it is not about coordinate, independent or equal power status of the two levels of government. What is of useful empirical interest is the degree of dependence and

---

[64] Nwabueze, *op. cit.*, p. 22 See also Wheare, *op. cit.*, p. 55

autonomy of the state governments in federal system.[65]

Isawa Elaigwu, another informed student of Nigerian government and politics, impressed by and accepting K.C. Wheare's view that "if we are looking for examples of federal government, it is not sufficient to look at constitutions only. What matters just as much is the practice of government,"[66] and drew attention to the cruciality of "the working of the [political] system" as a basis for pronouncing on whether or not it is federal.[67] There is considerable merit in this procedure for evaluation, which will be adopted and followed in the remaining body of this analysis, now that the foregoing conceptual analysis has demonstrated conclusively that there is absolutely no doubt that the principle of federalism and the concept of military rule are antithetical and incompatible.

General Ibrahim Badamasi Babangida became President, Commander-in-Chief of the Armed Forces of the 'Federal' Republic of Nigeria on 27 August 1985, following a successful overthrow of General Mohammadu Buhari. The Armed Forces Ruling Council, which he headed, supervised the conduct and management of Nigerian affairs for eight years until General Babangida 'stepped aside' on 6 August 1993. General Babangida ruled Nigeria with great political skill and dexterity, but plunged the country into an unparalleled depth of institutionalized corruption and a structural adjustment programme without a human face. It was widely believed that he had a hidden political agenda and an amazing capacity to keep the

---

[65] Oyovbaire, *op. cit.*, p. xvi

[66] Wheare, *op. cit.*, p. 20

[67] Elaigwu, *loc. cit.*,

Nigerian public guessing about what his political intention was. But, more relevant to the central hypothesis of this essay is that, like his immediate predecessor, his administration, in practice, killed and nailed the coffin of federalism in Nigeria.

The first point that needs to be made and emphasized is that federalism cannot be the appropriate political grid to which authoritarian military governance could be congruently anchored. Which explains why it became imperative that General Babangida's Decree No. 17 of 1985 should further retain, albeit in an amended form, General Buhari's Decree No. 1 of 1984, which had suspended and modified the most fundamental provisions of the *Constitution of the Federal Republic of Nigeria, 1979.* Decree No. 17 of 1985, which wholesomely purged the federal spirit, impulse or essence out of the 1979 Constitution and replaced it with what amounted to a prefectorial alternative could not, to say the least, have constituted an appropriate constitutional foundation for the operation of a federal polity in the country. It did, however, successfully synchronize and congruently align the newly fabricated and peremptorily imposed legal order with the authoritarian, hierarchical and centralized impulses of military governance. Federalism consequently became the first victim of Decree No. 17 of 1985 precisely because of the structural incompatibility between it and military authoritarianism.

The institutional structure and political processes of governance under the military regime of General Babangida transparently violated the traditions associated with the practice and culture of federalism. Isawa Elaigwu would seem to have trivialized the importance and substance of the structural difference between democratic and authoritarian culture of support for federalism, and has therefore merely put his fingers and addressed only the tip of the huge iceberg when he suggested that:

> ...the major difference in the operations of federalism under civilian and military regimes in Nigeria are to be found in the style and structures of administration.[68]

The differences are more fundamental and substantive than this observation would suggest.

Under General Babangida, the principal actors involved in the authoritative allocation of values in the country belonged to the same constituency and professional class, the military. A few of them were self-appointed; all others were appointed by the self-appointed praetorian guards. And given the command/obedience structure of the military establishment and its deep veneration for hierarchy, the political heads of the component states in Nigeria between 1985 and 1993 were appointed by General Babangida and the Armed Forces Ruling Council (AFRC) at the centre. Strictly speaking, they were on military posting as military governors of the component states of the Nigerian polity. Again, given the vertical relations of command and obedience in the Armed Forces, military governors were responsible and accountable to General Babangida, President, and Commander-in-Chief of the Armed Forces, who appointed them in the first instance. Since their postings as military governors of the component states, as well as their removal or redeployment, were at the *discretion* and *pleasure* of the 'federal' military government, the superimposition of military rule on a

---

[68] Ibid.

federal political landscape was quite naturally and expectedly bound to change the character of the political order and to automatically transform the Nigerian polity under General Babangida to a species of prefectorial administration notwithstanding the refusal of the new 'federal' military government to admit this. As Robert C. Fried has reminded us,

> ...[t]he essence of a prefectorial system is that it establishes a personal representative of the [central] government in every locality - a single official who represents, can speak for, and commits all departments of the central government.[69]

Given the unity of command which is a distinguishing feature of any military organization, it is quite understandable why "the essence of prefectorialism is personification of the national government in the province."[70] Admittedly, prefectorialism means hierarchy, but it is more than centralization, which is a generally recognized trend in many political systems, including federal systems. In the words of Daniel Elazar, "prefectorialism has to do with the way in which things are imposed and forced and managed. That's the difference."[71] The well-known answers to important questions like: who, between 1985 and 1993, appointed the military governors of the states; to whom were they responsible and

---

[69] Robert C. Fried, "Prefectorialism in America?" *Publius: The Journal of Federalism*, Vol. 11, No. 2 Spring 1981, p. 24

[70] Ibid.

[71] Daniel Elazar, "Prefects, Pragmatism and Practice: A Response to the Respondents", *Publius: The Journal of Federalism*, Vol. 11, No. 2 1981, p. 56

accountable; and who controlled them certainly injured the integrity of the crucial principles of 'autonomy'. 'separateness' and 'mutual non-interference' which underpin federalism.[72]

Under General Babangida, the institutional structure of decision-making at the centre was dominated by professional soldiers occupying strategic military posts. Regrettably but quite understandably, it was not designed to, among other things, articulate, protect and accommodate the *federal* qualities of the society and specifically to protect state interest, as one would expect in a federal arrangement. Decree No. 17 of 1985 established three major organs at the national level for policy making: the Armed Forces Ruling Council (AFRC); the National Council of State (NCS), which included all the military governors of the states and some members of the AFRC, and the National Council of Ministers. Appointed by and accountable to the AFRC, military governors of the states arguably represented national community interests in the component states more than state interests in the national political arena. Which, in effect, suggests the limitation and structural weakness and deficiency of the National Council of State as an ideal forum for protecting the interest of *both* the 'federal' and state governments. As will soon become obvious, there are grounds to wonder whether the military governors of the states, given their lower and subordinate military ranks, vis-à-vis the members of the Armed Forces Ruling Council (AFRC) were in a position to participate autonomously and effectively in the exercise of the federal legislative power. Again, it is debatable whether the National Council of State, composed as it was, could have been in a position to properly safeguard the interest of the

---

[72] Nwabueze, *op. cit.*, ch. 1

states if and when such interest conflicted and collided with that of the central government, especially in the context of a centralized unitary style of leadership and administration typically associated with military regimes.

Admittedly, the composition of General Babangida's National Council of Ministers paid formal deference to the 'federal character' principle in the 1979 Constitution. Nevertheless, even if one ignores what, in a different context, Ben Nwabueze called a 'lack of fidelity to the federal character principle' arising from the 'strategic departments and functions of government being concentrated among ministers and advisers from a particular section of the country,[73] it is arguable that the National Council of Ministers during the Babangida administration, was neither conceived nor did it operate as a guardian and protector of all conflicting sectional interests of the various ethnic publics in the entire Nigerian political community. And, as a matter of fact, the composition of the AFRC, 'the military substitute for a legislative body', did not reflect the federal character of the nation, and could not have been 'representative', given the provisions of Decree No. 7 of 1985 which established it and the assertion credited to General Babangida that, as far as the Military was concerned,

> there is no north, there is no south, there is no middle belt and...there is no religion. There is Nigeria and a Nigerian nation...In the military, we don't think of religion...promotion, postings and performance are based purely on merit.[74]

[73] Ibid., p. 369
[74] *Newswatch*, 22 January 1990, pp. 11 & 16, cited in Ladipo Adamolekun, John Erero and Basil Oshionebo, "Federal Character'

The structure and management of inter-governmental relations between 1985 and 1993 provide perhaps the most revealing indicator of the true character of General Babangida's so-called 'federal military government'. With respect to the political and administrative processes of governance which emerged during that period, certainly the most revealing and authoritative inside account is that provided by Admiral Aikhomu, Chief of General Staff/Vice-President and second-in-command to General Babangida. It deserves to be quoted comprehensively:

Throughout the life of this administration, military governors were on military posting and were thus required to take directives from the central administration. First, the Office of the Chief of General Staff (CGS) maintained close supervision of state military governors. And when in the course of the implementation of the presidential system, the Office of the Vice-President (VP) was brought into being in September 1990, the responsibility for supervising state military governors devolved on the Vice-President. As a control measure, yearly budget guidelines were issued by the Vice-President to the military governors who were subsequently physically present at the headquarters to defend their budgets. Financial data were also regularly and mandatorily obtained from the states, and quarterly returns on actual income and expenditures from the States were called for and received so as to inform subsequent sectional polity directives. In addition, monitoring teams went from the Office of the CGS/VP to the states to assess how faithfully the state governments implemented federal government directives and guidelines as well as the performance of the budgets. Also in accordance with true military principle, defaulters were duly penalised. During the era of military governors, the [National] Council of State comprised only the President, Commander-in-Chief of the Armed Forces, the CGS/VP, Service Chiefs and military governors themselves. At this forum, policy issues affecting the states were discussed and determined, with the states required to comply faithfully with Council conclusions. This was not all.

State and local government relationship with the federal government was further regulated by circulars of general application. These were mainly issued from the Office of the CGS/VP...In consideration of the above, federal measures tended to detract from the independence and autonomy of states even in areas where state and federal governments had concurrent powers. States tended to lose their distinct identities as the effective second tier of government. These developments lent strength to the impression of a 'unitary State' of Nigeria instead of a federated union. But as far as the military government at the centre has been concerned, federal measures were designed to ensure uniform standards, shore up similar levels of performance as well as provide equitable opportunity in terms of conditions of services while envisaging national direction and purpose.[75]

The indisputable nerve-centre of vital decision-making was General Babangida's supposedly 'federal' government which was in full eagle-eye and hierarchical monitoring as well as centralized control, direction and shaping of the political, legislative and administrative-behaviour of the

---

[75] Aikhomu, *loc. cit.*, pp. 51-52

other tiers of government, especially as a presumably because the understanding of General Babangida's military administration was "to use the advantages of centralized military administration to weaken the prospects for a confederation."[76] It was not so much the centralizing trend that worries students of Nigerian federalism in so far as all federal systems experience this pattern of development. What worries them was the centralized and hierarchically-structured style of governance and administration which virtually reduced the military governors of the states to mere *agents* and *prefects* of General Babangida's federal military government. In effect, as stated elsewhere, under General Babangida

> the pattern of intergovernmental relations flows, strictly speaking, less from the formal constitutional allocation of legislative responsibilities but more from the practical neo-imperial, and command-and obedience relationship between the superior military officers at the federal level and their subordinate colleagues who exercise what amounts to delegated authority at the state level.[77]

The fact that, under military rule in Nigeria, the autonomy which states still retain was, as one scholar pungently and incisively put it, the autonomy to carry out federal policies differently"[78] not only precisely reflects the collapse, decay and atrophy of federalism as the constitutional principle on which the Nigerian political

---

[76] Ibid., p. 45.

[77] R.A. Akindele, "The Conduct and Management of Intergovernmental Relations: The Limits of Information and Experience Sharing by Students of Federalism and Students of International Affairs," *Nigerian Journal of Federalism*, Vol. 1, No. 2 December 1994, p. 16

[78] Aikhomu, *loc. cit.*, p. 53

system between 1985 and 1993 was supposed and claimed to have been anchored but also draws attention to the core-periphery model of intergovernmental relations that existed under General Babangida.

Admittedly, the environment of intergovernmental relations in the country between 1985 and 1993 was modified slightly but significantly from 1990 to 1992 by two steps in the promised progressive disengagement of the military from governance at the state level. The first step was the appointment of civilian deputy governors in August 1990; the second was the subsequent emergence of elected civilian governors. But neither of the two steps individually nor both of them collectively put the state governments in a position which could, by the logic of true federalism, be considered as befitting and appropriate to them. The seemingly endless transition to civil rule and democratic governance in Nigeria under General Babangida certainly did not rescue the state governments from the suffocating control of the federal military government in imperial claws and suffocating control of the federal military government in Abuja, although one has to admit that while "[w]ith democratic civilian administration in place on the states, the ascendancy of a federated nation of states where no part can be greater than the whole is not in doubt,"[79] the speculation as to "whether the military designed a period of dyarchy so as to be able to fish for a provocative confrontation with politicians in order to postpone indefinitely the handing over of power"[80] was very much

---

[79] Alex Gboyega, "Protecting Local Governments form Arbitrary State and Federal interference: What Prospects for the 1990s?" *Publius: The Journal of Federalism*, Vol. 21, No. 4 Fall 1991, p. 45

[80] Rotimi T. Suberu., "The Struggle for New States in Nigeria," *African Affairs*, Vol. 90, No. 361. See also by the same author, "Recent

around at that time and indeed attracted and commanded respectability in some quarters.

Under General Babangida's military regime, there were two seemingly popular decisions which had mixed blessings but certainly some bearing on the integrity and survival of federalism. One was the creation of more states and local governments;[81] the other was the promotion of the autonomy of local governments vis-à-vis the state governments.[82] As President, and Commander-in-Chief of the Armed Forces, General Babangida presided over a federation consisting of nineteen states in 1985. Two years later, in 1987, two additional states were created, thus increasing the number to twenty-one. In 1991, additional nine states were constituted, making a total of thirty states in the federal polity. The publicly articulated intention of the state-creation exercises was to respond to the wishes and pressures of territorially grouped and significant minorities for self-determination and government. But the military elites who believe that a marriage of federalism and military governance is possible even if it inflicts definitional injuries on and to the concept of federalism cannot but be aware of Adele Jinadu's observation that "the more states that are created, the less autonomous or less viable such states will be in relation to the central or centre

---

Demands for New States in Nigeria," *Nigerian Journal of Federalism*, Vol. 1, No. 2 December 1994, pp. 67-82

[81] O.O. Oyelakin, "State-Local Government Relations under the Military, 1985-1992," *Nigerian Journal of Federalism*, Vol. 1, No. 1 June 1994, pp. 21-32; Gboyega, *loc. cit.*,

[82] L. Adele Jinadu, "Federalism and the Structure of Nigerian Federation: Some Recurrent Issues," *Nigerian Journal of Federalism*, Vol. 1, No. 2 December 1994, p. 63 See also Larry Diamond, "Issues in the Constitutional Design of a Third Nigerian Republic," *African Affairs*, Vol. 86, 1987, p. 21

government."[83] It is arguable that this awareness was one of the unarticulated reasons which predisposed the Babangida regime to rush, as it were, to effect state-creation twice between 1987 and 1991. With its "concomitant emasculation and immiseration of state...authorities," as Rotimi Suberu puts it,[84] "the creation of more states under the military has sounded the death-knell of state governments."[85] The consequential implication of the continuing proliferation of states has been succinctly summarized as follows by Dele Olowu: "[t]he real problem, however, is not small state units but the strong centralized federal system, particularly the concentration of resources in the federal government."[86] This is, as also rightly argued by Adele Jinadu, both the cause and effect of the considerable erosion and decline in the autonomy of state governments directly but partially attributed to state creation.[87] To General Babangida, creating more states was as much a strategy of structural transformation aimed at reducing the imbalance in the federal system and thus ensuring stability as it was of enhancing the power and status of the federal military government in Abuja. In any case, if as it is sometimes argued, "enhanced autonomy for the state is best guaranteed by democratization and

---

[83] Rotimi T. Suberu, "Recent Demands for New States in Nigeria," *Nigerian Journal of Federalism*, Vol. 1, No. 2 December 1994, p. 67
[84] L. Adele Jinadu, "Federalism and the Structure of the Nigerian Federalism Some Recurrent Issues," *Nigeria Journal of Federalism*, Vol. 1, No. 2 December 1994, p. 63
[85] Dele Olowu, "The Literature on Nigerian Federalism: A Critical Appraisal," *Publius: The Journal of Federalism*, Vol. 21, No. 4 Fall 1991, p. 161
[86] L. Adele Jinadu, *loc. cit*, p. 63
[87] Ibid.

demilitarization,"[88] it could not have been realized under the dictatorial and authoritarian regime of General Babangida who, on three occasions, annoyingly and provocatively aborted the transition to civil rule and democratic governance, until he was compelled to 'step aside', in disgrace as it were, in August 1993.

General Babangida's military regime did its best to promote and institutionalize the autonomy of local government's vis-à-vis the state governments, having tried very hard to advance, cement and legitimize the conception of local governments as a distinct third tier of government in the country's political system. With effect from July 1988, it adopted the policy of direct statutory funding of local government, thus bypassing the state governments through which such allocation was previously passed and consequently preventing them from hijacking and diverting such funds to other uses; it raised the local governments share of statutory allocation from the Federation Account from 10 per cent 15 per cent in 1990 and to 20 per cent in 1992 in order to strengthen the fiscal capacity of the third tier of government; and abolished the state ministry of local government replacing it with departments of local government affairs in the Governor's Office to assist and advise, but not to control, local governments within the state.[89] Progressive and commendable as these administrative reforms were, they neither constituted the central challenge and core problematic of federal-state relations nor addressed the fundamental issue of the vertical character of intergovernmental relations and of the hierarchical subordination of state governments to the

---

[88] See Oyelakin, *loc. cit.*, p. 25; Gboyega, *loc. cit.*, pp. 55, 57.

[89] Aikhomu, *loc. cit.*, p. 11

federal government under General Babangida's military rule. What the reforms did was to strengthen local governments, the weakest link in the system, at the expense of the state governments; and given the place of local governments at the periphery and as the outermost circle in the concentric circle paradigm of governmental power structure in Nigeria, the effect of the reforms was to strengthen the status and position of General Babangida's federal military government as the imperial nerve-centre of action in Nigeria's political system.

The constraining impact of General Babangida's military rule on the vitality and dynamics of the federal experiment in Nigeria deserves further consideration on two fronts. First, since the military and police officers appointed to govern actually and monopolistically interpenetrated the highest echelons of the two major levels of government under the Babangida administration, the political pattern and dynamics of intergovernmental [federal-state] relations between 1985 and 1993, as they were under General Buhari, quite understandably showed greater inclination and emphasis towards programmed, institutionalized and mechanical *co-operation* than towards *conflict, competition* and *rivalry* among governments. According to Admiral Aikhomu,

> [i]n the Nigerian federal setting, the understanding of the Military Administration is that various tiers of government are designed as related parts of a Nigerian government system, to be characterized more by cooperation and shared functions than by unnecessary conflict and unhealthy competition.[90]

---

[90] Ladipo Adamolekun and John Kincaid, "The Federal Solution: Assessment and Prognosis for Nigeria and Africa," *Publius: The Journal of Federalism*, Vol. 21, No. 4 Fall 1991, p. 180

Thus, by concentrating on and emphasizing only *one* dimension, type or pattern of intergovernmental military rule under General Babangida suffocated the growth and flowering of the full dynamics of inter-governmental relations typically associated with mature federal political systems. Healthy conflict, rivalry and competition among governments in federal politics are intrinsically and essentially functional for the vitality and sustainable growth and balanced development of any federal system of government, and must therefore, neither be discouraged nor inhibited in any federation, as was the case under General Babangida's military regime. The point needs to be made that neither rivalry nor competition can be said to be inimical to cooperation, for:

> [l]ike competition in the marketplace, competition among governments can promote the interdependence ordinarily needed to build cooperation. Furthermore, the translation of destructive conflict into constructive competition requires, itself, an act of cooperation, an agreement to structure a federal political order that permits liberty and self-government.[91]

The second front on which attention must be focused in coming to grips with and explaining the surreptitiously programmed death of federalism in Nigeria under General Babangida is the *authoritarian* environment and hierarchical structure of military rule. Both in theory and practice, "[w]hile democracy can prosper without federalism, federalism cannot exist without democratic pluralism which permits groups really to be autonomous."[92]

---

[91] Duchacek, *loc. cit.*, p. 14
[92] Ibid.

But, simply put, General Babangida was dictator; and dictators do not and cannot tolerate active oppositional politics and open dissent, no matter how constructive they are. Authoritarian regimes may be benevolent; they may occasionally be responsible to the aspirations of the people as perceived by them. They are not responsible and accountable to the people who, in any case, neither put them in power nor have structured means of ensuring and enforcing the vital values of responsibility and accountability which democracy venerates. General Babangida's Decree No. 17 of 1985 retained the dissolution of democratic institutions in General Buhari's Decree No. 1 of 1984 which constituted, in an amended form, the principal Decree for his [Babangida's] military administration. The guided democratic experiment he embarked upon in his seemingly endless transition to civil rule and good governance was, to say the least, half-heartedly pursued and implemented, arguable because of his intention and hidden agenda to succeed himself as president of a post-military government. The hands of elected civilian governors at the state level were considerably tied in the management and conduct of the affairs of their states, while it was common knowledge that public funds were massively used by the federal military government illegally to buy-off and curry the favour of the elected National Assembly in an apparent search for support to abort the transition to democratic civil rule. Civil society, which constitutes the bedrock of any democratic dispensation, was not permitted to grow and function luxuriantly. An oppressive regime hostile to human rights and fundamental freedom was put in place and nourished. Many decrees, often with retroactive validity, were put beyond challenge and contestation in any court of law, while Babangida's military government itself very often failed to obey decisions of the courts against it. Executive lawlessness and high-handedness characterized the regime between 1985 and 1993. Quite understandably but regrettably, the non-democratic environment and dictatorial dispensation under General Babangida did not provide a conducive climate of support for the vitality of the principle of federalism and practice of federal government. The truth is that authoritarian military rule under General Babangida killed federalism in Nigeria; after all, is federalism not "a territorial dimension of true *democracy*?"[93]

Concluding remarks

Theoretical explication of the concept of federalism and military rule quite conclusively shows that both of them are antithetical and, strictly speaking, flow in parallel streams which logically cannot meet. But how, then, could Babangida's military regime, 1985-1993, justifiably call itself 'Federal Military Government', and be so regarded? Military federalism is clearly a huge conceptual joke, a misnomer that misses or glosses over the huge difference between the concepts of non-centralization and centre-periphery when applied rigorously to the structure of power distribution in a political system.

An analysis of the practice and working of the so-called federal experiment in Nigeria between 1985 and 1993 under General Babangida also leads us to the conclusion that when a centralized and command-

---

[93] See Tunde Adeniran, "The Two-Party System and the Federal Political Process," *Publius: The Journal of Federalism*, Vol. 21, No. 4 Fall 1991, pp. 31-44

structured style of administration falsely masquerades itself around as a military government clad in a glaringly mismatched federal gown, it lays itself open to a huge credibility and identity crisis. There was only one *ruling* party in Nigeria between 1985 and 1993, which was the military. It was cohesive and hierarchically organized. Its officers interpenetrated the central and state levels of government as decision-makers. The military created two political parties, the National Republican Party (NRC) and the Social Democratic Party (SDP), drew up for them their manifesto, funded them generously, registered and launched them and finally dissolved them when they became irrelevant to its bidden political agenda.[94] The authoritarian political culture which it designed and over which it presided, and the 'suffocating centralist structures' which accompanied it, did not and could not, allow federalism to survive, let alone to grow luxuriantly. There is no empirical and conceptual justification or basis for the nomenclature of federal military government often used to describe military rule in Nigeria, including and particularly military rule under General Babangida, 1985-1993, for:

> [t]he fundamental truth that emerges from practical, operational experience in governance in Nigeria is that military rule and federalism are incompatible...stripped of its spirit, essence and vitality, federalism remains massively strangulated and endangered under military rule.[95]

---

[94] R.A. Akindele, "Nigeria in the Global Market of Experiments in Fedralism," in J. I. Elaigwu and R. A. Akindele (eds), *op. cit.*

[95] J. Bayo Adekanye, *Military Occupation and Social Stratification*, (Ibadan: Vantage Publishers (Int.) Ltd., 1993), p. 31

The fundamental explanation for the incompatibility of federalism and military rule is rooted in and flows from the fact that, reared in the professional and occupational culture of command and obedience, military officers, as ruling elites who presumptuously regard themselves as '*the* one unifying force in the country' and are now generally perceived as 'the most privileged occupational group in the country,'[96] do not, and cannot, 'think federal'; and unless they 'think federal', they cannot 'act federal'; but, as Daniel Elazar, among others, has reminded us, "the maintenance of federalism involves 'thinking federal'."[97] Without it, federalism withers away, as it actually did during the military regime of General Babangida in Nigeria, 1985-1993.

---

[96] Ibid.
[97] Elazar, *op. cit.*, p. 192

Malthouse Monographs on Africa

Editor: Dafe Otobo, DPhil (Oxford),
Professor, University of Lagos, Lagos, Nigeria

Advisory editorial board

Malthouse Monographs on Africa

Malthouse Monographs on Africa, new on the scene, are peer-reviewed works on Africa covering the six main areas of a) social sciences and development studies; b) history, law and international relations; c) environmental and agricultural studies; d) gender, refugee and conflict studies; e) strategic and defence studies; and f) labour and trades unions.

The Monographs are intended to provide an arena for free contestation of ideas and as outlet for research and empirical studies on Africa in the areas indicated above. The monographs thus have no links with, nor funded by, any African government or political party. Nor do the views expressed in them represent those of the editorial board

Works for consideration may be of purely theoretical, or historical or applied in nature or policy-oriented. Such may be sent directly to the Series Editor as electronic files (dafeotobo2002@yahoo.co.uk) in Microsoft Word Rich Text format, or to the publishers (malthouse_press@yahoo.com}. Diskettes and hardcopies may also be sent to the publishers at the address on the imprint page. The aim is to publish accepted works within three months.

Malthouse Monographs on Africa
Volumes 1 – 9

Guest Series Editor: Dayo Oluyemi-Kusa,
Director, External Conflict Prevention & Resolution,
Institute for Peace and Conflict Resolution, The Presidency,
Abuja, Nigeria

- Rotimi T. Suberu, *Institutional structure and process of government in Nigeria, 1985-1993*
- R. A. Akindele, *Federalism under General Babangida's administration in Nigeria*
- Dele Olowu & Kunle Awotokun, *Local government and the IBB administration*
- Cyril Obi, *The Nigerian private sector under adjustment and crisis 1985-1993*
- Bola A. Akinterinwa, *General Ibrahim Babangida's legacy: the domestic and international dimensions*
- Nereus I. Nwosu, *Nigeria's foreign policy under General Babangida*
- Antonia T. Oko-Osi, *Corruption and corrupt practices: institutionalization and legitimation under the Babangida Administration*
- Oyeleye Oyediran & Babafemi Badejo, *The military and democracy in Nigeria: the Political Bureau Report*
- Adekunle Amuwo, *Politics of the annulment of June 12 presidential election in Nigeria*

Malthouse Press Limited
43 Onitana Street, Off Stadium Hotel Road,
Surulere, Lagos, Nigeria
E-mail: malthouse_press@yahoo.com
malthouse_lagos@yahoo.co.uk
Tel: 01-773 53 44, 0802 364 2402

© Malthouse Monographs on Africa 2007
First Published 2007
ISBN 978 023 238 9

Distributors:
African Books Collective Ltd
Email: abc@africanbookscollective.com
Website: http://www.africanbookscollective.com

Guest Editor's comment

All the Monographs in this series attempt to explore and document events, policies and impact of the General Ibrahim Babangida-led military regime in Nigeria, covering the period 1985 to 1993. These contributions were originally for a book edited by me on that regime but other considerations, especially that of comprehensiveness of coverage of arguably the most momentous phase in Nigeria's post-Civil War socio-political development, led to the shelving of that idea. It was thought that a more useful scope or coverage might be achieved through a continuing development of Monographs on different facets of Nigerian society under this regime – a feat which may only be possible in a book so voluminous and whose cost might be such as to be out of the reach of the intended audience.

I should like to thank all the contributors who have waited this long to see their work in print, a fate that is unlikely to befall the contributors of the other titles currently in preparation. I am grateful to the publishers for including these titles in Malthouse Monographs for Africa family.

Dayo Oluyemi-Kusa

Local government and the IBB administration

Professor Dele Olowu
Department of Public Administration
Obafemi Awolowo University, Ile-Ife,
Nigeria

&
Dr Kunle Awotokun
Department of Public Administration
Obafemi Awolowo University, Ile-Ife,
Nigeria

No. 3

Contents

Introduction   83
The 1976 local government reforms   85
Babangida and local governance   90
Babangida and state/society reforms: DFFRI,   91
The Better Life Programme   93
Babangida and the community banks initiative   98
People's Bank   101
Further reforms of the local government system   102
Babangida and primary health at local level   105
The 'presidentialisation' of local governments   106
Babangida and the two-party system government system   110
The NRC and SDP   111
Conclusion   113

Introduction

> I would like to assume that, by now, the
> commitment of the present administration to
> grassroots developments is no longer in doubt.
> Even more so, I would like to assume that the
> generality of the citizens of this nation now
> recognise that this administration has done far
> more for grassroots development than any other
> government in the history of this country.
> (Babangida, 1990).

Since the colonial period, local governments have been regarded as critical institutions for democratisation and economic development. In the immediate post-independence years, they were relegated in terms of their relevance to these two central concerns of the Nigerian state. However, beginning from August 1976, their importance and relevance in respect of Nigeria's drive for democracy and economic development were reasserted.

In the regime alternation between civilian and military political leaders since independence, some patterns had begun to emerge in respect of the attitude of military political rulers and their civilian counterparts to the development of local government. First, the military authorities generally tended to be more favourably disposed to the development and strengthening of local governments than the civilian politicians. Secondly, not all-military administration favoured the enhancement of local government. Generally, military governments regarded the reform of local governments as part of their re-civilisation or democratisation programmes. Hence, if a military government was not committed to a determined transition to civil rule, it was not likely to be interested in the development or strengthening of local government. For instance, the global reform of local government in 1976 was part of Murtala/Obasanjo's five-point plan of re-civilisation and democratisation. In contrast, neither Gowon nor Buhari/Idiagbon regimes paid much attention to local government, again because they had no clear programmes of re-civilisation.

From this point of view, therefore, it is a tough task placing the Babangida administration in terms of local government. On the one hand, he came up with a robust plan to transform Nigerian politics into one that is devoid of the failure of the past by asserting the grassroots character of Nigerian politics. To this end it took a number of steps to further entrench the local government reform and to make them autonomous of state government control and to transform local economic conditions through a number of central government initiatives. On the other hand, it seems as if the Babangida reforms ended up making the local governments even more heavily dependent not on the people but on the federal government. Such a development led not only to alienation from the grassroots but also provided even greater avenues for graft and corrupt practices at the local government levels. Increasingly, local government chieftains increasingly became pawns in the hands of an adroit military politician determined to hold on to power at all costs. This latter predisposition seems to have held away in the latter half (1990-93) of the Babangida years.

In this chapter, we take a look at these two contradictory tendencies as they relate to local government. First, we shall examine the philosophy of local government revitalisation as developed from 1976 onwards. Secondly, we shall review the claims of the Babangida administration and contrast this with the performance of his government as far as local government and grassroots development was concerned in the first half (1983-89) and in the latter half of the Babangida years. Finally, we shall attempt to interpret the data in the light of our analysis.

The 1976 local government reforms

1976 is generally regarded as a watershed in the history of local government in Nigeria. It was a period when concerted efforts were made on the part of the central government to accord this unit of governance (local government) its pride of place in the scheme of things in the country. As the authors of this reform had noted:

> Local governments have over the years suffered from the continuous whittling down of their powers. The state Governments have continued to encroach upon what would normally have been the exclusive preserves of local Government.[98]

It was against this background that the military government of Murtala/Obasanjo made a determined effort to strengthen the local governments as a way of engendering democracy and socio-economic development. Indeed the objectives of the reform contained among others these two important elements. It states, *inter alia*,

(i) to increase me responsibilities of local authorities by a process of decentralisation that ensures that appropriate divisions of functions exist between state and local

---

[98]Federal Republic of Nigeria, *Guidelines for Local Government Reform* (Kaduna, Government Printer 1976) p.1

governments and that local authorities thereby play a significant role in the development process;

(ii) to ensure that participation and involvement begin at the grassroots level since local authorities are very close to the people, they are most favourably placed to understand and appreciate the peoples' demands. Local authorities should hence, serve both input and output functions within the system. They should articulate the demands of the masses and when these are satisfied within the limits of available resources, they should provide authorities with the necessary feedback.[99]

The effort to democratise and decentralise local governments, is perhaps, the most salutary effect of the 1976 local government reforms. This can, perhaps, be better appreciated against the background that hitherto, 'civilian politicians in the regions (states) particularly disliked democratically elected local government because of pockets of opposition emerged in the larger cities such as (Ibadan, Lagos, Kano) for the *de facto* single-party regimes they had imposed in each of the three regions'[100] It is needless to retort that oppositions are essential ingredients for a sustainable or enduring democracy. The inability of the ruling parties to accommodate and recognise them had inflicted an incalculable damage on our body politic.

---

[99] Background paper entitled 'Local Government system'': Proposed Reforms and Role of Traditional Rulers citing Supreme Council Memo. (References SMC 7 (73) 3 and Ncs (74) Prepared by the Cabinet Office, Political Division, n.d., 12 page.

[100] Dele Olowu 'Local Institutions and Development: The Nigeria Experience' in Edward G. Goetz and Susan E. Clark (eds.) *The New Localism: Comparative Urban politics in a Global Era* (London, sage Publications Inc, p. 155.

Indeed the 1976 reforms entrenched the concept of representative democracy as a national norm.[101] It states, *inter alia:*

> The system of local government by democratically elected local government councils is under this constitution guaranteed; and accordingly the government of every state shall ensure their existence under a law which provides for the establishment, structure, composition, finance and functions of such council.[102]

Be that as it may, the second variable under our consideration is the conciliatory role which the local government were meant to play in the socio-economic development of the nation as a whole. With the steady increase in the per capita income of Nigeria resulting from oil-boom and Arab oil crisis between the mid-1970s to 1980s, the federal military government of Murtala/Obasanjo conceived the reorganisation of local government as a potential instrument for ensuring that the accumulated resources percolated to the mass of the people. In other words, the 1976 local government reform was partly meant to address the problems of rural poverty through the provision of social infrastructures and at the local level. The guidelines on the reform pontificated:

> These reforms would mean nothing if they did not include the certainty that as from now, every stratum of Nigeria society would benefit from the

---

[101] Alex Gboyega 'Local; Government Reforms in Nigeria' in Philip Mawhood (ed.) *Local Government in the Third World: the experience of Tropical Africa* (Chichester, John Wiley & sons 1985) p. 235.

[102] Federal Republic of Nigeria the 1979 Constitution of Nigeria (Lagos, a Daily Times Publication, 1979) Sec. 7(I).

> continued prosperity of this country, through the availability of amenities indeed, necessities, such as electricity, adequate water supply, improved transportation, health facilities and so on.[103]

The reforms therefore proceeded to create a range of functions which were meant to be performed by the local government. The functions was divided into two categories those exclusive to local governments and those in which they were to participate in concurrently with the state government:

1. Exclusive

The main functions of a local government shall be as follows:

a) formulation of economic planning and redevelopment schemes for local government area:
b) collection of rates and insurance of radio and television licenses;
c) establishment and maintenance of cemeteries, burial grounds, and homes for the destitute or infirm;
d) licensing of bicycles, trucks (other than mechanically propelled trucks) canoes, wheelbarrows, and carts;
e) Establishment, maintenance, and regulation of slaughter houses slaughter stabs, markets, motor parks and public conveniences;
f) Construction and maintenance of roads, street lighting, drains, parks, garden, open spaces, or such public facilities as may be prescribed from time to time by the military governor or house of assembly of a state;

---

[103] Guidelines for Local Government Reforms, *op. cit.*, p. 11.

g) naming of roads and streets and numbering of houses;
h) provision and maintenance of public conveniences, sewage and refuse disposal;
i) registration of all births, death and marriage;
j) assessment of privately owned houses or tenements for the purposes of leaving such rates as may be prescribed by the military governor or house of assembly of a state;
k) control and regulation of:

     i)   outdoor advertising and boarding
     ii) movement and keeping of pets of all descriptions;
     iii) shops and kiosks;
     vi) restaurants, bakeries, and other places for sale of food to the public;
     v) licensing, regulation, and control of the sale of liquor.

2. Participatory

The functions of a local government shall include participation of such government in the government of a state as respects the following matters, namely:

a) the provision and maintenance of primary, adult and vocational education;
b) the development of agriculture and national resources, other than the exploitation of mineral;
c) the provision and maintenance of health services; and
d) such other functions as my be conferred upon a local government by the military governor or the house of assembly.[104]

---

[104] Ibid.

In all, the gains of the 1976 local government reforms can be viewed in a number of ways. It brought about uniformity in the level of governance at the local government level. It also ensured the transfer of resources from the centre to the periphery, this can be better appreciated against the general critique that 'government expenditures tended to be excessively centralised and were either urban oriented or skewed along ethic lines.'[105] This has led to equalitarian (if not egalitarian) policy in the distribution of resources among the various units of local government in Nigeria. It has also helped in building basic social infrastructures throughout the country. The gains of the reforms had been so concretised that other regimes that have emerged in the political scene ever since 1979 when the Obasanjo regime handed over power to civilians, have not only sustained the reform but used it as a basis for fashioning out other political and administrative changes, the Babangida regime inclusive.

Babangida and local governance

Babangida was not just concerned about local government, but about improving the lot of the ordinary person. Local governments were therefore, only one of the mechanisms of bringing about this realisation. Hence, especially in its earlier period, it sought not only to reform the mechanisms of local government, but also to carry out a number of structural economic reform aimed at improving grassroots economy. The other variant has to do with various political reforms at the local government level such as the

---

[105] Dele Olowu, *op. cit.,* p. 160.

cancellation of ministries for local government at state level, abolition (though reversed later) of local government service commission (LGSC) to pave way for local government autonomy, direct payment of revenue accruing to local governments from the federation account, direct election, institutionalisation of two grassroots democratic parties, intergovernmental relations, etc. However, it will be instructive to state that owing to the limited space accorded to us in this volume, we shall only concern ourselves with the most important reforms, of the period. We shall start first with state/society oriented reforms. Our analysis will not necessarily follow historic sequence.

Babangida and state/society reforms: DFFRI

President Ibrahim Badamosi Babangida in his New Year broadcast in January 1986 intimated the nation with his plan to constitute directorate for food, roads and infrastructure (DFFRI) which was going to be based in the presidency. By 1987 the membership and a decree establishing it had had been made public.[106]

In specific terms, the enabling decree gave twenty-four functions to the directorate which included:

> The identification, and support of local community organisations for rural development activities, the identification and support of high food and fibre production; the creation of national feeder road network (through construction, improvement and maintenance activities); and liaison with appropriate federal, state and local government

---

[106] Federal Government of Nigeria, Decree 4, of 1987.

councils for the provision of water, health facilities, electricity, communication service.[107]

In order to execute all these functions, all levels of government (i.e. federal, state and local) were also involved with each of them constituting its own directorate or committee as the case may be.

However, a cursory examination on the activities of DFFRI showed more concentration on the rehabilitation of earth roads at the expense of other functions which were meant to be performed by the directorate. Not only were most of the roads seasonal but also their rehabilitation had brought DFFRI in direct confrontation with the people at the local level, who resented the idea of DFFRI mounting a signpost to a road not initiated by it.

It can be thus inferred that the DFFRI initiative was not people-inspired but rather, a top-bottom approach to the issue of development. This model was doomed to fail as it was not in reality with human instinct. Most of the infrastructures so created could not withstand the test of time. For instance 'some of the water pumps constructed by the directorate are known to be of poor quality and difficult to maintain by the people.'[108] Indeed, many boreholes project were abandoned by the directorate because of inability to reach the water table. In addition many successfully commissioned boreholes were known to have collapsed or "cave in" owing to lack of hydrological survey.

---

[107] Dele Olowu, 'Institutional Approaches to Rural Infrastructure Development in Nigeria,' *Quarterly Journal of Administration* (QJA), Vol. xx, 3 & 4, April/July 1986 p. 169.

[108] Ibid.

Another area of department of DFFRI was the weak institutional machinery set up by the federal government to measure performance and expenditure of its fund. The team was known as report and monitoring department. Many (if not all) states were known to have given it (the team) false of their activities in order to secure greater discretionary funds from the federal government. It was an open secret that most of the roads claimed to have been constructed by DFFRI had been in existence for several decades before the conception of the directorate. There was also the problem of inability to secure adequate funds from the federal government by the directorate. This had, in turn, culminated in the inability of DFFRI to realise its noble objectives.

In theory there is no doubt that DFFRI was a well conceived programme to ameliorate the condition of poor people at the grassroots, but the implementation, as our analysis had shown above was poor.

This programme (DFFRI) had a twin-sister known generally as Better Life for Rural Women Programme (BLFP).

The Better Life Programme (BLFP)

The Better Life for Rural Women was initiated by the wife of President Babangida in 1987. Like its DFFRI counterpart, the initiation was borne out of concern over mass poverty that has pervaded the nation generally and the rural womenfolk in particular. The whole essence of the programme was to see how best to maximise the productivity of rural women for their own development. In addition, it was also targeted at evolving ways of improving the condition of women within the context of their cultural and religious persuasion. It was for this reason that the author of the programme, Mrs Maryam Babangida, said:

> Women in rural areas deserve our primary attention and consideration because they indisputably form the backbone of the rural economy in contemporary Nigerian society. In perspective too, from the pre-colonial economy to contemporary times, they have consistently been an indispensable factor forming an integral vital and often a dominant part of our peasant and rural economies, firmly establishing themselves in the area of farming, food production, distribution, marketing and trading. Accordingly, in this period of accelerating change it is in the vital interest of us all to explore and consolidate strategies for enhancing their participation and contribution to our economy.[109]

In a nutshell the programme as conceived above was meant to pool the physical and intellectual resources of rural women into measurable contributions towards the country's development. The programme was also meant to sustain rural development through self-sufficiency in food production. It also sought to ameliorate socio-economic and technological development of the rural populace in the country, hence the conception of cottage industries as an integral part of the programme.

---

[109] An address presented by the then First Lady Mrs Maryam Babangida at a symposium held to mark the International Women's Day 7th March, 1990. See also *Nigeria Tribune* (Ibadan) March 22, 1990. P.1.

Operational strategies

In order to realise the laudable objectives of the programme, a number of strategies were adopted throughout the nation such as public enlightenment campaign, involvement of government establishment of directorate of women affairs and task force.

In the bid to ensure appropriate recognition for the programme, the then First Lady, Maryam Babangida mobilised the wives of the state military governors to actively support it at the state level. The wives of the governors were also expected to mobilise the wives of chairmen of local government, in turn, for same purpose. The policy makers at the three levels of government were also directed through presidential fiat to give financial as well as moral support to it.

The government involvement as a strategy could be seen from its subventions and donations, for instance, the National Directorate of Employment (NDE) announced a donation of ₦2.4 million in 1989 for the execution of BLFP.[110] In the same vein the DFFRI through its chairman Air Vice Marshal Larry Koinyan announced the incorporation of BLFP to its activities.

There was also the establishment of the National Women Commission at the federal level. Directorates of women affairs were instituted to give impetus to the initiative. Each of the directorates at state level was meant to co-ordinate the various women programmes such as education, health, cottage industries, etc. Ad hoc task forces

---

[110] O.C. Ketitu, The Contributions of the Better Life for Rural women Programme in Akure Local Government Ondo State, MSc project Department of Local Government Studies, OAU, Ile-Ife, May 1992 p. 52.

were also set up in all the states to monitor and ensure the implementation of its various programmes.

Activities of the BLFP

During the period in question a number of activities were engaged in by the agency. Some of them were visible in the rural areas - e.g. cottage industries co-operative societies, agriculture, nutrition, health programmes, education, training workshops, social welfare services, market outlet, assisted projects, etc. All these were essential components of the BLFP. Their degree of success varies from state to state. One thing was certain that the rural women were given imputes to boost their productive capacity at the local level. Of particular note was the assistance generated from the United Nations Fund for Population Activities christened 'women affairs development project'. The components of the project were adult literacy for rural women. Income generation and integrated family health services. As a result of this, machines, equipment such as gari processing and presser, grains mill, rice mill and palm oil processing machines were provided in form of loans to rural women.

The BLFP also embarked on intellectual and skill development for the womenfolk. Induction courses, workshop and skill acquisition through vocational training were adopted as strategies to enhance the production capacity of the women in rural areas. It is interesting to note that most of the training of rural women had been in the area of evolving simple indigenous but modern technologies in food processing, preservation and packaging. This stemmed from the fact that most of food produced in rural areas has been wasted after harvest due to improper processing, preservation and storage facilities.

Constraints of the programme

Indeed some of the constraints that faced the BLFP were rooted in the variegated cultures of the Nigeria populace. For instance, some cultural or religious beliefs have qualitatively and progressively reduced womenfolk to subordinate positions. As a result not much can be done within the time frame of BLFP to liberate these group of women who themselves must have resigned to fate.

Many of the men folk at the rural area had also viewed the activities of BLFP with disdain. Some of them felt that such a mobilising programme was designed to make their wives less dependent and consequently insubordinate or incorrigible. This again must be perceived from the traditional conception of the role of men as masters and breadwinners. The non-inclusion of men folk at the conception stage was a monumental and tactical weakness of the programme. This had largely made its good intention to be misconstrued by the rural men folk.

Since the programme is government inspired, it meant that the lion share of its fund had to come from the federal government. The economic and fiscal problems being faced by the federal government of the period owing to global oil-glut had limited the scope of activities of the programme. It was such that most of its centres the supposed centres of learning lacked basic infrastructures such as electricity, water, serviceable vehicles to aid mobility and right calibre of women and materials to galvanise change in the rural areas.

The most persistent constraint of the BLFP is the
phenomenon of rural and urban elites among the
womenfolk who had virtually hijacked the programme and
converted its gains to their own advantages; thereby
aggravating the already worsened situation of the rural
women. In other words, the target groups (potential
beneficiaries) were estranged by the educated women, and
this was the noticeable trend all over the federation.

Babangida and the community banks initiative

By 1986, the global economic recession had spelt doom for
the generality of people of Nigeria; this economic distortion
had led to adoption of a structural adjustment programme
otherwise called SAP. Owing to this economic hardship
the then federal government was faced with two critical
questions. First, how can it mobilise capital to provide for
small scale producers majority of whom reside in the rural
areas. The second question was how government can
ensure that such credit being provided will be repaid
promptly.[111]

By January 1 1990, President Babangida made known
the intention of his administration to embark on 'a novel
system of community banking.'[112] Community bank is 'a
self-sustaining financial institution, owned and managed by
a community, for the purpose of providing credit, banking

---

[111] Akin L. Mabogunje The capitalisation of money and credit in the
development process: the case of Community Banking in Nigeria'
African Journal of Institutions and Development (AJID) Vol. 1,2,
1995 p. 10.

[112] Ibid. p.10

and other financial services to its members, largely on the basis of their self-recognition and credit worthiness.'[113]

The community bank (CBs) are expected to be owned and financed by the generality of the people in a community. Such local institutions as community development associations, co-operative societies, farmers' unions, trade groups, etc., are normally encouraged to have substantial share in its establishment. The CBs differ considerably from the commercial and merchant banks in the sense that they are not expected to carry out sophisticated banking service such as foreign exchange transactions, letters of credit, corporate financing, equipment leasing, etc. They are allowed to operate basic banking purchase and sale of securities to raise and sustain their capital base.' [114]

In all, the government expect CBs to:

a) inoculate disciplined banking habits in the rural population;
b) inspire in the communities the spirit of ownership and maintenance of facilities and organisation;
c) generate credit from within the communities for enhancing the development of productive activities and the purposeful improvement of the economic status of the communities and their individual members;
d) provide bridge loans during off-seasons as a means of breaking the dependency on, and the hold of local money-lenders on the vast majority of rural dwellers;
e) formalise the use of communities as effective vehicles of rural change and national development;

---

[113] 16. National Board for Community Banks, *The Community Banking System in Nigeria*, (Abuja, 1992) 0.11.

[114] Ibid. p. 11

f) generally promote rural activities such as agriculture, commerce, arts and crafts, agro and mineral based cottage and small-scale industries, vocational and trade skills, rural transportation and other rural economic activities, particularly in support of small farmers, micro-entrepreneurs, women, youths and co-operatives; and

g) promote the emergence of an effective and integrated national financial system that responds to the needs of the whole economy, from the grassroots to the national level.[115]

In a recent survey of impact of CBs in investment patterns at the local level carried out by a research group called local   institution   and   socio-economic   development (LISDP);[116] the workings of CBs have been on the average commendable. To date, there are well over 1,500 CBs spread all over the country with more than 70% of them located in rural areas. As its founding chairman, Professor Akin L Mabogunje, observed:

> ...within the very limited period of its existence, CBs are already making a significant difference in credit provision to a large number of small-scale producers   whether   in   farming,   trading, transportation or craft activities.'[117]

CBs have also reduced the activities of traditional money-lenders in the rural areas with its attendant problems on the

---

[115] Ibid., pp. 11-12.

[116] See, *inter alia*, D. Olowu and O.L. Oludimu, Impact of Community Banks on Investment Patterns in Niger: An Overview', in *AJID*, *op. cit.*, pp. 16- 88.

[117] Akin L. Mabogunje, *op. cit.*, p. 12.

mass of the people to the barest minimum. CBs have already assumed the position of promotional agencies for local economic sustenance. It is hoped that there will be opportunities for workshop where the peasants will be taught and encouraged to take loans to boost their economic activities. This is because some of them still perceive borrowing, even for business purposes in a negative light. It is only by so doing that money and credit can be capitalised in the rural sector.

Peoples' Bank

The Peoples' Bank, like CBs, was established principally to alleviate the sufferings of the people. However, unlike the CBs, it is limited in terms of its number of outlets. Initially, the bank provided maximum credit facility of ₦2,000 for an individual at a time. The federal government jacked up the maximum ceiling to ₦5,000 when it was discovered that ₦2,000 was grossly inadequate to meet the needs of the people.

Peoples' Bank branches are few and far between to make much impact in the lives of the people. Indeed its disposable resources are few as the federal government admits that 'a large segment of the population requires a higher level of credit than the Peoples' Bank can accommodate.'[118]

---

[118] National Board for Community Banks, *op. cit.*, p. 10.

Further reforms of the local government system

The second segment of our discussion has to do with the various reforms which affected the local government as a tier of government. The most popular one at the inception of Babangida's administration was the abolition of the state ministries for local government. With the 1976 local government reforms, the state ministries for local government had become increasingly unpopular with the Political functionaries as well as administrative officials in the local government councils. One of such allegations that was brought against them was unnecessary delay that always greeted the approval of their budgets. Indeed, when Dasuki panel went round to gather information for its report, all the local government officials throughout the federation called for the abrogation of the ministry. It was not surprising therefore that the federal government of Babangida abolished it in 1988. It was replaced by the "directorate of bureau of local government and chieftaincies matters" in the deputy governor's office. Even though the directorate is meant to serve as 'information clearing house for local government as well as render other technical assistance to local governments.'[119] The general observation was that the exercise was just a change of name as the old habits continues under the bureaux.

---

[119] Sylvanus Ikhide *et al.*, USAID Governance Initiative in Nigeria: A Strategic Assessment of Primary Health Care and Local Government (Lagos, USAID Affairs Office 1994) p.6.

Direct payment of federal allocations

Another salutary reform of the local government under Babangida regime was the direct payment of monthly revenue allocation accruing to local government from the federation account. Hitherto the state governments were known to have been hijacking the federal grants to local government. The idea of hijacking the local government allocation came with civilian regime between 1979 and 1983 and that was almost the practice throughout the federation, except Lagos State.

Not only did Babangida made direct payment to local government his regime witnessed steady increase of local government revenue allocation from 10 per cent to 15 per cent in 1990 and by January 1992 it had increased to 29 per cent. It is instructive to note that state government allocations from the same fund dropped from 34 per cent to 24 per cent while the federal government retained 50 per cent.[120]

Creation of new local governments

Some 301 local governments were created with the 1976 local government reforms, no sooner were these created than agitation for more local governments emerged. Many of the agitators based their argument on the fact the present ones were too large to bring government nearer to the people. Many resented the location of the headquarters of these councils. The civilian government (1979-83) had met the aspiration and yearnings of the people by doubling or tripling their number in some states, but these were reversed by the military junta of Buhari/Idiagbon in 1984.

---

[120] Ibid., p. 6

By 1987 Babangida administration started creating new local government with the creation Katsina and Akwa Ibom states. Between 1990 and 1991 a total of 593 local governments had been created.

Administrative reforms

Following the 1988 civil service reform, the federal government of Babangida decided to extend the reforms to local governments in order to bring them at par with their federal and state counterparts. With the designation of minister and commissioner at federal and state respectively as chief executive of their executive of their ministries, chairmen of local governments were also designated as chief executive and accounting officer. This was a marked departure as secretaries to local government were hitherto designated as chief executive and accounting officer.

In addition to this, a new organisational structure was approved for all local governments in the nation. All local government councils were to have six functional departments. These are administration; personnel management; finance and supplies, planning, research and statistics; education; agriculture and national resources; works, land and survey, medical and health. However, there were four optional departments, namely, personnel management, education, health and agriculture.[121]

By these reforms, the office of "the director of local government audit" was created. The reforms also insulated

---

[121] S. B. Ayo, Evolution of the Nigeria Local Government system, in A. M. Awotokun, (ed.) *New Trends in Nigerian Local Government*, Ile-Ife, Obafemi Awolowo University Press 1995) p.5

the office of the auditor from civil service control; he (the auditor) is only answerable to state house of assembly or military government in case of military regime.

Another re-organisation embarked upon by Babangida administration is the setting up of "local government alarm committee" to prevent local government functionaries from incurring illegal expenditure on behalf of the council. The local government internal auditor is expected to play a crucial role in this regard. By the reform, anybody could raise the alarm, once raised, no payment could be effected until a panel comprising the director of local government audit and others have investigated the matter.

Babangida and primary health care

By 1988, Babangida regime articulated a new national health policy. 'The focus of the policy was a community-based health system in which primary, secondary and tertiary health care are organised at local, provincial and national levels, with each mutually supporting the other.[122] As far back as 1986, a total number of 52 model local government areas (LGAs) had been selected as pilot project sites, for the purpose of strengthening PHC at LGA level. Each of these 52 LGAs was linked with a university teaching hospital or school of health technology for the purpose of training their health officials.

Under the PHC programme state government were asked to devolve all PHC responsibilities to local government over a three-year period terminating on June 30, 1990. However, the states government were still saddled with the responsibilities of supervising and co-

---

[122] Ibid.

ordinating PHC activities; as well as playing an advocacy role.

In all, PHC activities revolve around ten core functions:

i) public education;
ii) improvement in nutrition;
iii) adequate safe water and basic sanitation;
iv) maternal and child health care, including family planning;
v) immunisation;
vi) prevention and control of endemic and epidemic diseases;
vii) provision of essential drugs and supplies;
viii) elderly and handicapped care; and
ix) accident and injury care.

In this programme, the peasants were carried along, as they constituted the district and village health committees. The committees' input was in the form of providing information, suggestions for improvement, complaints, control, etc. By this programme, Babangida was supposed to have brought health care delivery to the doorsteps of the mass of people.

The 'presidentialization' of local governments

The philosophy of "presidentialization" of local government by Babangida administration was anchored on the need to change the orientation of the public bureaucracy from the Westminster model (parliamentary), which is

British in origin, to that of presidential democracy in consonance with Nigerian constitutions of 1979 and 1989. This inevitably implied that the apparatus of government which hitherto had been organised along parliamentary model must give way to the presidential innovation. The idea of presidentialising local government is based on the concept of separation of powers. The doctrine (separation of powers) as propounded by Montesquieu connotes that separation of powers allows for specialisation in governmental process. It is such that powers are shared among the three arms of government, viz. legislature, executive and judiciary. The legislature is expected to make the law, the executive to execute the law made by the legislature. In addition, the executive is expected to be responsible for the overall administration of the state, while the judiciary arm is to ascertain the constitutionality of the legislative and executive proposals. The judiciary also mediates in event of crisis or conflict between the legislative and the executive.

Under the reform in question, the councillors constituted the legislative arm, while the executive branch consisted of the chairman, vice chairman, and secretary to the local government, supervisors as well as administrative units of the local government.

The guidelines issued from the office of the then vice-president empowered the legislative arm of the local government with such functions as:

Law making, debating, passing local legislation, approving amending and possibly criticising local government annual budget, vetting and monitoring the implementation of projects, examining and debating monthly statements of income and expenditure, advising, consulting and liaising with

> local government chairman who is the chief
> executive in the local government chairmen who is
> the chief executive in the local government
> system.[123]

From all indications, the basic rationale for introducing the doctrine of separation of powers at the local level was to ensure uniformity of governance among the three levels of government. As the then Vice-President Augustus Aikhomu said: "...this will be in consonance with the constitutional requirements and practice at the federal and state levels under the civilian rule."[124] The arrangement was to provide checks and balances among the organs of government to modify the strict separation of powers as no organ of government can operate in a watertight compartment. Each branch of government is meant to check the power of the other when the need arises. In other words, the theory "assumes no branch will be able to act free from all restraints and tyranny will be avoided."[125]

The experience of the period was such that the crop of councillors so elected did not check the official excesses of the executive. What they did in most cases was to resort to blackmail in order to force their way through the executive. Indeed, there were lot of impeachment threat in the bid to make executive succumb to their financial demand. As O. Oyelakin observed:

---

[123] Federal Government of Nigeria Local Government Basic Constitutional and Transitional Provisions (Amendment) Decree 23, Official Gazette, Vol. 78, 25, 24th June 1991.

[124] Ibid.

[125] E. Michael Toye and Kingsley Igweike, *Introduction to the 1979 Constitution* (London, Macmillan Press 1982) p. 134.

> Some legislative arms of local governments are now said to be dangling the threat of impeachment over the heads of certain local government chairman like the sword of Damocles. In many cases, this is reportedly being doe to coerce the affected chairman to part with one favour or the other.[126]

Indeed one can safely assume that impeachment clause was not employed to punish the offenders for offences so committed but as a tool for resource allocation. In fact, an analysis of legislative-executive relation at local government, need take cognisance of spatial as well as vertical dimensions of what Richard A. Joseph called ethno-clientelism.[127] Without such an understanding, one cannot grasp the ease with which the societal resources were being appropriated by the executive without the legislator bringing them to book. Clientelism and broadly ethno-clientelism provide the linkages between the legislature and the executive arms of government in which the essential functions or roles to be performed each are blurred and inconsequential as long as individual group interest are served.

The various legislative houses at the local government level then were talking shops. Any chairman could be unaccountability and irresponsible as   he/she wished provide the financial and material demands of the legislators were met. As L. Adamolekun observed:

---

[126] O. Oyelakin Implementation of the Executive Federal Presidential system of Government at the Local Government Level: Its Logic, Merits and Constraints,' in A. M Awotokun (ed.) *New Trends in Nigerian Local Government, op. cit.*, p.50.

[127] R.A. Joseph, *Democratic and Prebendal Politics in Nigeria: The rise and Fall of the Second Republic* (Ibadan, Spectrum Books Ltd, 1991) p. 55.

> What pre-occupied the legislators was different
> from the ideals of enforcing accountability and
> promoting responsiveness. A political executive that
> was willing to be responsive to the   personal
> (usually) financial) interest of legislators could be as
> irresponsive and unaccountable to the mass of the
> population as it wished.[128]

The issue of accountability and administrative responsiveness was at its lowest ebb during the period. It is that it made nonsense of what could have been the gains of the presidency in relation to the reform in question.

Babangida and the two-party system at local level

Babangida administration, in his first effort to reintroduce party politics, promulgated Decree 25 of 1987 which aimed at those contesting elections at local government level. The decree prevented the "old politicians" from participating in the elections.   By the legal exclusion of 'old breed' politicians from the political process of the time, Babangida administration felt that the 'new breed' would emerge to sanitise the political system.   It was also felt that by so doing the situation would provide 'a recruitment channel for the political leadership of the Third Republic.'[129]

---

[128] L. Adamolekun, "Accountability in Governmental Administration since Independence" A Contribution to the First Distinguished Academic and Professional Guest Lecture Series. Sponsored by the Nigerian Institute of Journalism (NIJ) April, 1985 p. 11.

[129] Tunji Olagunju *et al., Transition to Democracy in Nigeria*, 1993 (Ibadan, Safari Books Ltd 1993) p. 208.

The Babangida administration worked under a serious pressure owing to the exclusion of the so-called 'old-breed' politicians, such that when the ban on politics was lifted the President had to disbar or "unban" them. Many critics felt it was a panicky measure on the part of the administration. About fifty political associations sprang up with only thirteen filing their applications for registration with the national electoral commission (NEC). All of them were eventually proscribed thereby giving birth to the formation of National Republican Convention (NRC) and Social Democratic Party (SDP) by Babangida regime.

The NRC and the SDP

These two political parties were tagged "grassroots parties" by the presidency. By grassroots it was meant that the membership and leadership of the parities would originate from the ward level which incidentally is the smallest unit of the country's political organisation,[130] since the ward was regarded as the nerve-centre of parties organisation, the intended party members were expected to join the political party of their choice at the ward branch office in which they reside. Another intention was that through the local government the party structures and hierarchies would aggregate upward to the state and federal levels.

    The idea of a government forming political parties for the people had been roundly criticized as undemocratic imposition'[131] on the mass of the people. The government responded that the aim was to force political associations to

---

[130] Ibid., p. 221.

[131] O. Oyediran and A. Agbaje, "Two-partyism Democratic Transition in Nigeria," *Journal of Modern African Studies*, vol. 29, 2, 1991.

be national in outlook, by virtue of membership spread criterion and compel them to reflect the democratic ethos of participation and accountability in their organisation structures and hierarchies.[132]

By our own judgement, the two parties did a lot of havoc to the body politic of the local government. Before 1990 local government elections, a lot of factions had developed within the rank and file of the two parotids leading to mutual; suspicion among the people who had hitherto regarded themselves as their "brother' keepers". Because the formation was not people-inspired, the people did not have a sense of absolute commitment to them. Indeed they were structurally fragile and functionally redundant. In many wards membership register were not available and in places where they were available their authentic nature was questioned by party members and factions.[133] Branch meetings were not held regularly and far between. The parties could not direct their membership to pay up their dues owing to intra-parties hegemonic rivalries. The hierarchies of the parties too did not make any concerted effort to collect them because of the huge public funds being injected in the form of grants by the federal government. At a more critical level the urge to mobilise party membership for additional resources was stultified because the executive of the two parties lacked moral courage in that they had little or nothing to show for the 'manner in which the take-off grants were being disbursed.'[134]

---

[132] Tunji Olagunju *et al., op. cit.,* 212
[133] Ibid., p. 222
[134] Ibid., p. 219

In a way, it is reasonable to contend that the intra party factionalism had further alienated the parties form the ideals of participatory democratic principles which Babangida administration had initially conceived. Furthermore the debilitated position of NRC and SDP as at the time of General Abacha's take-over has not vindicated the theory which informed the design of the parties as a panacea for national cohesion.

Conclusion

It sounds plausible to conclude on a note that Babangida regime paid more attention to local government reforms and grassroots development than any other regime in the country to date. The later was carried out through a number of structural and economic reforms aimed at improving grassroots economy as we have demonstrated above.

In explicit term, it will be more apposite to assess the contribution of Babangida administration two phases. The first phase (1986-1990) witnessed a period of consuming passion for the improvement in the quality of life of the peasants. Then, the Babangida administration was bent on removing the forces that were creating and sustaining their backwardness.

However, for every step made forward in the first phase, the administration made two steps backwards in the second phase. The public sentiments became tilted against the regime owing to endless transition programmes to the extent that people became suspicious of every intention of the regime. The political environment soon became hostile and not much could be said in favour of the regime. The regime had to resort to a kind of defence mechanism in its dealing with the public. The aetiology of this crisis can be located squarely on the theory which states that military as an undemocratic institution cannot bring about democracy. The inability of the Babangida administration to hand over to an elected government has obliterated his good intentions.

Finally, it is more reasonable to maintain that Babangida's gains in grassroots development were mixed and, perhaps, pyrrhic.

www.ingramcontent.com/pod-product-compliance
Lightning Source LLC
Chambersburg PA
CBHW021835020426
42334CB00014B/640